From Broken to Beautiful

A Journey to Restore a Shattered Self-Image

Manda Hall

Editor: Nancy J. Dorsett, Polishing Prose

Cover Art: RavSingh via Fiverr.com

Dedication

To the hurt, broken, shattered woman who is looking for hope, inspiration, encouragement and restoration beyond the brokenness of her past.

To the woman who wants to look in the mirror and see past all the ugliness and rejection of her life.

I am opening my heart and soul for you! I am exposing the hurt, broken and shattered woman I used to be, to give you hope, inspiration and encouragement that comes with being able to look in the mirror and see the beautiful, confident, empowered woman God has waiting for you through restoration and transformation.

A Note About This Book

My Beautiful Friend,

I can't tell you how honored and excited I am for you to read this book. It is because of you that my story is being told. God has placed on my heart all His beautiful daughters who are experiencing pain, brokenness and shattered pieces of their self-images and lives.

God has led me on an incredible, painful, maturing, restorative and transformative journey. I have taken many steps forward and a few backwards on my way out of a deep, dark pit of depression. I will share with you the keys that led me to my transformation. Since early in the process, I have documented in my journal my experiences, prayers, questions, concerns, fears and dreams. I will be sharing portions of my journal with you; they contain very raw emotions and thoughts I experienced on climb out of the pit. I hope by sharing my story, you will be encouraged and inspired that no matter how flawed and broken you are, you, too, can emerge out of the darkness. You can live in God's light as the beautiful, confident and empowered woman God created you to be!

Writing in my journal was a big part of the restoration process for me. To get you started journaling, I will be posing challenging questions to get you to pause, think and then write. As you thoughtfully answer these questions, you will begin your own journey from Broken to Beautiful.

My prayers, God's unconditional love, mercy, grace and forgiveness, will cover you when you make the courageous decision to leave behind the darkness of the pit of lies and walk toward the light of your new, restored life in the Truth. Today is the day to make that decision!

With Grace & Blessings,

Manda

Contents

1 Falling Into the Pit

Picture yourself driving down the freeway when suddenly a rock slams into your windshield. You hear the loud crash and you watch as cracks radiate out from the point of impact. The cracks become larger and longer until your view becomes obstructed. Like rocks smashing into your windshield, the words and actions of others coupled with your own negative thoughts can cause your heart to shatter. Every unkind word, every thoughtless action directed toward you, breaks you a little more. The cracks in your heart and soul become so numerous that your view of yourself gets distorted. Is there any way to get rid of the cracks and restore a clear and accurate view of yourself? The answer is an absolute, "Yes!" Decades of deep cracks had severely damaged my self-worth and devalued the quality of my life, but I have experienced such a restoration of my heart and soul that I hardly recognize who I am! Let me share with you the amazing and miraculous transformation that took me on a journey from broken to beautiful. But first I will share how a lifetime of rocks caused the deep cracks in my heart and soul sent me falling into the deepest, darkest pit.

As a little girl, I always wanted to fit in, but I just felt like an ugly duckling. With short hair and lots of freckles, I played dress up and with dolls in hopes that I would not feel like what I was--a tomboy. Through my teen years, I desperately tried to fit in by being either the class clown or know-it-all, but the popular kids continued to ignore me. All the while I struggled with school. I appeared tough on the outside, but I was a broken, hurt, and sad little girl on the inside.

When I reached high school, I thought that I had a chance to start over; there were so many more people and I could find my place. Sports seemed to me to be a place where being a tomboy would be valued, but I did not make any of the sports teams I had tried out for my freshman year. However, I fell in love with volleyball and decided to become the best volleyball player I could be; I never missed making the team again. Being vertically challenged at 5 feet, 4 inches, it was an uphill battle; but I found my niche as a setter. When I was playing I felt good about myself, and being a know-it-all about the game was a huge benefit. I finally felt like I belonged.

Yet something else happened that reinforced my sense that I was different. When I was a sophomore in high school, my mom was diagnosed with breast cancer. Less than two years into remission, her body was not strong enough to fight the cancer anymore; she passed away the summer before my senior year of high school. Another big rock, another deep crack.

I had a great group of friends, mostly guys, because I felt like I could relate to them since I was a tomboy and sports enthusiast. But I still felt like an ugly duckling. I wanted so desperately to be noticed; I wanted to feel pretty, like a girl. Finally my friend, Jason, noticed me (after my many attempts to get his attention) and I was starting to feel like a girl. I was no longer just a tomboy, I was more than a friend. After high school, I was expected to go to college; I knew that it was not going to be at all easy. My struggles with reading, which had plagued me through all my school years, caused me such difficulty that I was convinced to look elsewhere for my validation. College just wasn't for me.

Shortly after ending my college aspirations in a heap of failure, my high school boyfriend, Jason and I discovered I was expecting. 20 years old and pregnant, we decided to get married. I was in what would be my unborn daughter's room when I was approached by a family member who decided to share with me some information about my mother. In a moment something was revealed that rocked my entire world; it explained some of my past and changed my life forever. "You know, your mom was the same age when she had you. She wanted to have an abortion, but it was illegal. She was too scared to go to Mexico." An enormous boulder hit me, shattering my heart and soul. This knowledge was too much for me to bear. So I choose to bury that truth deep in my soul in hopes that I would forget what had been said. What better way to bury it then by shoving it down with food.

During my pregnancy I gained 60 pounds; but 60 pounds remained after I had my beautiful daughter. Less than two years later, when I became pregnant with my son, I added another 40 pounds to my small frame. My weight gain was halted by the birth of my son, who arrived 11 weeks early. The feelings of joy and happiness that should have surrounded his birth were overcome with the devastating thoughts that my son might die due to something I had done wrong. Broken and shattered again.

To ease the pain and to fill the emptiness I felt, I turned to my favorite coping mechanism-- food. Eating allowed me to ignore all the instances that had broken me down; food buried the memories deep away in my soul. The 100 pounds gained during my pregnancies, plus some more, served to cover up my deeply broken and painful past. By August 2004, I topped the scales at 253 pounds on a 5 feet, 4 inch frame. I was fat and I would soon learn I was dying. Being overweight made feel ugly and unworthy of love or attention. The many stones that were thrown at me, which broke and shattered my heart from my childhood and youth, had followed me into adulthood. As an adult, all the negative thoughts that ran around in my head added more rocks which continued to break my already shattered soul.

Another life-changing moment came in a doctor's office. Desperation gripped my heart when the physician announced that if I didn't lose the excess weight, I would not be alive in 10 years. I was killing myself. I wouldn't see my children graduate from high school. I would miss their weddings. I would never hold my grandchildren. I would do to my children what my mom had done to me--I would leave them alone, without a mom. Another rock, another deep crack.

Staying alive would mean taking drastic measures. 120 pounds would need to come off for me to achieve a healthy weight and survive. Even though it was urgent that I start to lose the weight, I procrastinated a couple of months because of fear of failure. For years I tried every diet, exercise and pill to lose weight with little success. Ultimately I failed; more rocks, more cracks. I decided drastic measures needed to be taken. On August 4, 2004 I had gastric bypass surgery and my physical body would begin to change. Over the next year, I lost 80 pounds; after 6 more months, I was lighter by another 40 pounds. By carefully following my post-surgery diet and engaging in moderate exercise, I have successfully maintained that weight loss for over 11 years! You would think that with a great new shape and a healthier eating lifestyle, I would feel beautiful on the inside too. Unfortunately, I continued to struggle with my self-image. When I looked in the mirror, I still saw a hurt, angry, shattered, 253-pound woman staring back at me. I was still broken. My physical body looked beautiful by the world's standards, however my distorted view in the mirror only magnified all the shattered pieces of my heart and soul.

The extent of my deep brokenness was not fully revealed until August of 2014. My mind descended into the deepest, darkest place I have ever experienced. I reached a pivotal moment, a crossroads, when I had to choose between life and death. Would I swallow a bottle of pills to end this desperation (part of me really did want to just give in to the darkness; the pain would finally be over) or would I reach out for help one last time knowing that the only person who could save me was God? Reaching out one final time (or at least I thought), staring at the pill bottle and all the shattered pieces of my heart and soul that had come crashing to the ground, I expected and waited for God not to answer. Without warning, my heart was overwhelmed with a sense of hope that I have never felt before. I grasped the pill bottle and flushed the pills down the drain; yet there was still as mess of shattered, jagged pieces of my life lying all around me that needed to be cleaned up. This was the first of many occasions when I learned that God is faithful to those who reach out to him. In their greatest weakness, He proves His greatness and powerful strength. *2 Corinthians 12:9* *"But he said to me, My grace is sufficient for you, for my power is made perfect in weakness. Therefore I will boast all more gladly about my weakness, so that Christ's power may rest on me."* In my incredible weakness, full of hurt and anger at the bottom of the pit, His grace and perfect love were more than sufficient for me. Only later would I learn how the second part of this verse would transform my life. I will boast all the more gladly about my own weakness, sharing all those shattered pieces of my life, so that Christ's power may rest on me and on my God-given purpose.

Along the way, I have learned more about each of the jagged pieces and how He sustains me while He restores them. When the memories of hurt, anger, and pain threaten to overwhelm me again, I cling to verses from the Bible to keep me from falling back into the deep, dark pit. Yes, I still have moments when I feel overcome and overwhelmed; it is a daily, sometimes hour-by-hour, or a minute-by-minute struggle. In the moments of weakness, the Psalms are an inspirational place for me. King David's words, in his pain and struggle, can help me through my difficulties. *Psalm 34:18* *"The LORD is close to the broken hearted and saves those who are crushed in spirit."* When I started my journey, I asked God, "Why did you put me through this? Why did I have to have my heart and soul broken and my spirit devastated?" Have you by chance asked these same questions about your life? He assured me that these experiences were necessary to shape me into the woman He created me to be. It is because of the stones and the resulting broken, jagged pieces of my own life plus God's redemptive work that I am able to share with you how He is healing me. "It is for a time like this, my daughter," He said to me.

Psalm 51:17 "*My sacrifice, O God, is a broken spirit; a broken and contrite heart you, God, will not despise.*" Even in those moments when my broken spirit and heart were weighed down with questions and doubts, realizing that I could surrender them to Him and He would not despise me for it, gave me some peace. He sent His son to cover all of us in His unconditional love, mercy and grace.

Do you realize that you can bring your broken heart and crushed spirit to Him? Will you? Why?

_____

_____

_____

_____

_____

_____

He is waiting with outstretched arms, open hands, and tender love for His beautiful, wonderful daughter--you!

What are the broken and shattered areas of your heart and soul that God is calling to your attention?

_____

_____

_____

_____

_____

_____

Surrendering it All, Really?

The words "surrender" and "submit" felt like nails screeching slowly down a chalkboard to me. Mrs. Type A personality wanted to be in full control. I did not want to let go of my pain, my selfishness, my pride, my hurt, my anger, my, my, my... The word surrender, to me, in the beginning meant admitting to being weak, having to forgive, losing control, and giving into the will of other people.

What does the word surrender mean to you? Explain.

_____

_____

_____

_____

Early in my journey when I reluctantly decided to surrender all those shattered, jagged pieces of my heart and soul, I did it as a sort of test for God. Would He accept me for who I was? Would He gather up all my broken pieces and help me repair the damage? Was His love really unconditional? He gently proved again and again, and continues to show me today, that in each case the answer is "Yes". As I have moved further along in the journey of surrendering to Him (sometimes multiple times a day), I willingly offer myself to Him. He's proven to be faithful, merciful, and unconditionally loving throughout all my tests and challenges. I am now opening my heart to trust Him and His Word. I can rely on Him and surrender to Him all my doubts, pain, pride, and selfishness. He will show me how to move forward in His strength. *Ephesians 3:16-17* *"I pray that out of his glorious riches he may strengthen you with power through his Spirit in your inner being so that Christ may dwell in your hearts through faith."*

In order for me to surrender, I had to acknowledge each and every stone that caused the brokenness of my heart and soul, and reach out to God and ask for help. I had to let my walls come down and expose my hurt, my imperfection, my fear. I would have to become vulnerable and transparent to others, and especially to God. None of this even remotely sounded appealing to me. Most of all, I believed that neither God nor others would accept me if my shattered, broken life were revealed. *Luke 14:33*

(AMP) "So then, any of you who does not forsake (renounce, surrender claim to, give up, say good-bye to) all that he has cannot be My disciple." This verse has had a significant impact on me as I have moved step by step in developing my personal relationship with God. To discover and fully realize His purpose and plan for my life, I had to surrender, give it all up, and say good-bye to all of my rocks that caused the brokenness that was my life.

As I was beginning to learn to surrender it all to Him, I started to see Him point out scriptures to me to give me extra reminders. *Jeremiah 38:20-21"They will not hand you over, Jeremiah replied. Obey the LORD by doing what I tell you. Then it will go well with you, and your life will be spared. But if you refuse to surrender, this is what the LORD has revealed to me..."* God graciously revealed that if I surrendered to His plan and purpose for my life, He could show me His vision and the bigger picture. It's only been very recently that I started to see the bigger picture, because I am getting better at surrendering myself to Him.

"Your life will be spared," the verse says. Those words spoke deeply to me, because my life was being spared. In the deepest, darkest moments when I had considered taking my life, He rescued me. It took an act of God for me to finally surrender to Him; allowing my weakness, hurt and pain to be exposed, reaching out in desperation for His unconditional love and

salvation, and asking Him to help me turn my life over to Him. _Acts 11:21_ (AMP) reads, _"And the presence of the Lord was with them with power, so that a great number [learned] to believe (to adhere to and trust in and rely on the Lord) and turned and surrendered themselves to Him."_ This verse helped me to see His power. I started to believe, trust, and rely on the Lord; I had a sense that I could truly let go and surrender.

There will be moments in life, when the natural response will be to think that something is too small to trouble God with it. Or perhaps we let God know we've got this one and He can relax. I have done this on many occasions. God wants us to surrender it ALL, every little nook and cranny, every little tiny detail and thought. **_Everything_**.

Is there anything you think is too small or too easy to surrender to God? What?

_____

_____

_____

_____

_____

_____

_____

_____

Following on the journey that He is calling me to walk out, I must surrender myself, broken pieces and all. Sometimes it is a minute-by-minute situation when I have to ask Him to take my brokenness and forgive me. I am definitely a work in progress.

Can you surrender and give God all those broken, shattered, jagged pieces of your heart and soul? Why?

_____

_____

_____

_____

_____

_____

_____

What is stopping you from surrendering it all to God?

_____

_____

_____

_____

_____

_____

_____

_____

Risk Reaching Out

For those of you, like me, who are very independent or self-reliant, reaching out to God or others is not an easy task. It may even seem impossible. How scary it is for us to reach out without knowing if He or someone else will be there to grab our hand. Our experience warns us no one will be there. God provided circumstances and people that guided me to risk reaching out for help.

I found myself in an unfamiliar place in the beginning of 2012. I was an empty nester, floundering without knowing why, and still I hadn't hit rock bottom. I knew Jesus died for my sins and that He was my Savior; however, I wondered why He would ever want to have a personal relationship with me. I decided to take a little step and see if God could be trusted. I reached out to God and asked Him directly, "Why am I here? What is my purpose?" This was the test to see if He would be there to grab my hand? _Psalm 18:6_ *"In my distress I called to the LORD; I cried to my God for help. From his temple he heard my voice; my cry came before him, into his ears."*

Firmly he grasped my hand and He gave me a very small glimpse of His purpose for me. He revealed it in a most unlikely way—in an ordinary conversation I had with my husband. I simply asked him the same questions I had asked God about my life's purpose. He reminded me, "You love shopping for clothes. You love helping your friends and family shop and put outfits together. Why not start a business helping other people the same way?" What? Me have a business? That's crazy! After all, I was not like my business-savvy husband. Who in the world would even hire me to help them? Allowing my negative self-image to dominate my thoughts, I stood in my closet crying tears of doubt and fear. How could I even think of starting a business by doing what I loved? I didn't deserve that kind of joy. Why start something that was bound to fail and cause more heartache? I did not like at all that answer God had given me. So I decided to ask again (ok, really tell) God that His plan was not going to work and I'd rather have a different plan. His gentle response was "no" to my request. So He nudged me to start an outfit blog (along with a business) using pictures to detail my daily adventures in my closet. Again, I doubted God saying, "I hate to be in front of the camera. I am so ordinary and not pretty; I just see a broken, shattered, 253-pound woman. Why would anyone want to see me; I am not worth anything. I don't have anything to offer." Finally, I gave into His persistent nudge and put my excuses aside. If I tried His idea and it did not work, it would show God and me that the outfit blog was the latest failure in my extensive string of failures.

My *Dress With Purpose* blog was birthed in March of 2012. It was about the most awkward, uncomfortable, embarrassing thing I had ever done. My self-doubt kept shouting at me, "Manda, you are crazy for doing this!" My stubbornness compelled me to show God that He was wrong; the blog would fail. He firmly held my hand and I defiantly followed Him. He began to show me that through the blog, I was helping women by giving them ideas for outfits. I was showing them that looking good on the outside didn't have to cost a fortune. The bonus was that they were thanking me for inspiring them. God was graciously showing me how His plan was the right one for me, because the blog became a success. With the success of the blog, came success in my business. With a glimpse of hope, God would not have to pull me kicking and screaming to follow His will going forward, at least for a little while.

In August of 2014, having achieved a place of self-confidence, I decided to let go of God's hand. I could not have known the disastrous consequences that stepping away from Him would cause. All at once, long-lost memories, that I thought were buried so deep they couldn't be found, flooded my brain. One vivid memory took my breath away and I free-fell down into that deep, dark pit. I was transported back many years to my daughter's nursery where I had heard those words, "You should have been aborted." The feelings that I was unlovable, unworthy, and unnecessary had endured and they rose up to shatter and break me again. That is when it happened--the deepest, darkest depression of my life engulfed me.

I have shared the moment that I was at my crossroads, pill bottle (death) or reaching out to Him (life). *Psalm 37:40* *"The L*ORD *helps them and delivers them; he delivers them from the wicked and saves them, because they take refuge in him."*

Have you reached your crossroads yet? When you reach your crossroads, which will you choose life and restoration or brokenness and mere survival? Why?

_____

_____

_____

_____

_____

I spent months putting on my happy face mask for the world, while feeling overwhelmed by the pain and hurt that I had deeply hidden away over the years. Still God was working on me. For a long time, I wondered why God chose to reveal that particular painful moment to me. It was because He knew, that for me to truly receive what He had for me, I had to pick up each rock and each shattered, jagged piece of the hurtful pain of my past. I had to begin to see that I was worthy and wanted by Him. He is still showing me how to heal; I am still on a journey of transformation.

It's O.K. to Ask

I often wondered if reaching out was the same as asking for help, but my experience has taught me that they are quite different. First, I had to be willing to reach out in hopes that someone would be there to grab my hand; and secondly, if they were there, I had to be willing to ask for help. *Isaiah 7:11* *"Ask the LORD your God for a sign, whether in the deepest depths or in the highest heights."*

Is it time for you to reach out and ask for help? Why?

_____

_____

_____

_____

_____

For an independent, self-reliant woman like myself, asking for help was one of the hardest things to do. I knew "asking" for help meant that I would need break down the walls that I had so efficiently built up over the years and I would have to rely on someone else. But I had to take the risk, because being an independent and self-reliant woman had led to me to extreme loneliness.

First, I had to ask God for help; second, I had to rely on Him to be faithful. Imagine what a big leap of faith it was for a girl who hadn't been able to reach out for fear that no one would be there. I began to ask for His help, guidance, and knowledge. *Ephesians 1:17* *"I keep asking that the God of our Lord Jesus Christ, the glorious Father, may give you the Spirit of wisdom and revelation, so that you may know him better."* I had to have faith that His instruction and guidance would come in many different packages, but first and foremost would be in His Word.

As I shared earlier, school and reading have never come easy to me, so reading the Bible and studying His Word was not going to be easy. But as part of the redemptive process, God breathed into me a love for reading. It had been 25 years since I had read a book from cover to cover. I would always start with high hopes, but soon I would get discouraged and stop. I struggled with reading because the words on the page would start to blur. My disability led to labeling which made me feel that I was as unworthy as I believed. The word "disability" was another stone; broken again. I grew to resent reading when reading became harder, I convinced myself to hate it. Even though reading is still a struggle for me, God has empowered me to persevere. He has given me a new love of reading; He has rewarded me with many truths through His Word and through the words of Christian authors.

My journey began with The Book and a book entitled *The Circle Maker: Praying Circles Around Your Biggest Dreams and*

Greatest Fears, by Mark Batterson. The sub-title for this book really intrigued me; I gravitated to the words, "Greatest Fears". That is mainly because fear is something I have struggled with for so many years (see Living with the Voices). Sprinkled throughout the book are references to the power of prayer, and how to have "vision beyond your resources". He explains how seeing past our circumstances can lead us from fear to realizing our God-given dreams, which I will share in more detail with you in "Our Hearts Must Go On". For a woman who was consumed by fear and who had never really allowed herself to dream, it was the perfect starting place for me. God gave me the right book at the right time, and it was a game changer. It took me two months to read it all. I still had to battle through the blurry pages, and I found myself rereading page after page. Perseverance and God's help allowed me to finish the book and I treasure the truths I learned.

In what areas to you need to ask for help?

_____

_____

_____

_____

_____

_____

_____

_____

He has been so faithful to respond to my cries for help. Although His answers were not always the ones I expected or wanted, yet they were what I needed. I am learning that there are times when I still feel like saying, "God, I think I got this." But I remember that I can get lost; and without His constant help, I can get overcome with the vision of all those stones being hurled at me. Even when things are going well, I still need to ask for His help to get me though those moments.

There came a time when I finally realized that I needed to seek and ask for help from others. I couldn't just hide behind learning and gaining knowledge through books, which was much easier to do. Since I had hidden myself away from the world for 20 years and pushed everyone away, it was difficult to know who to go to for help. Sometimes family members are too close to you to be honestly helpful. At first, it was really hard; I had to learn to reengage in the world. I started attending church and participating in Christian women's groups to ask for the help I needed. Developing friendships was a new concept for me, but I met some really incredible ladies who showed me how to be a friend again. I now have women in my life who are personal mentors, spiritual mentors, as well as a Christian life and business coach who hold me accountable. They warn me when I am falling off the path, pick me up when I do fall, and they encourage me to keep moving forward.

Who do you have around you who could become a personal, mental and spiritual mentor to you? Make a list.

_____

_____

_____

_____

_____

_____

_____

I had endured so much pain, struggle, and brokenness. When I took a really hard, honest look at how much of a mess of shattered, broken pieces I really was, I knew that I had to look to God to put me back together. I faced a life or death choice and I choose life. I fully surrendered this broken heart and soul to Him. Day-by-day, minute-by-minute, He is putting all the broken pieces into the places He originally envisioned when He fearfully and wonderfully created me.

It is time for you to take that step of surrendering fully to Him.

Next, I had to let go of the fear that God was not going to be there when I reached out to Him. He showed me how He had always been there for me even when I let go and thought I could do it on my own. When I reached again for Him to save my life, He was there to love me and forgive me. God continually answers my prayers and my cries for help.

Lastly, I had to learn to ask for help, not only from God but from others. Asking God was much easier (yet still hard), then asking others. My past efforts and experience had made me feel unworthy to ask for help. Not only has God provided support through His words and the words of people, He has put the right people in my path to help me.

Let go, surrender, risk reaching out and asking for help!

Today I can look back and I can be so thankful for this continual process. Even when the hurt and pain, the despair and hopelessness seem overwhelming, I can trust Him. He is putting back all the broken pieces so I can become His beautiful daughter. I am so grateful that God led me to write my struggles, challenges, feelings, and victories in my journal.

2 *Writing Your Way Out*

A teenage girl is struggling to find her way through school, facing challenges to read, and the demands on her to excel in school. In order for her to receive love and the validation that she was worthy of that love, she had to meet and exceed the demanding expectations. She had failed over and over again, never measuring up or even coming close. Why in the world would she ever have the desire to read again, learn, grow or even write? Does any of this sound familiar to what you may have experienced in your life? It does to me, because this was me. God gave me the gift of the loving to read, even with the challenges, and then came the intense desire to learn and grow. Never in a million years did I dream or even have the slightest desire to write. Yet again, He began to change my thinking.

Sometime ago, before I started this journey from broken

to beautiful, I attended a seminar led and sponsored by my friend, Maria Keckler, author of *Bridge Builders, How Superb Communicators Get What they Want in Business and in Life,* and owner of Superb Communications. She was teaching on the importance of journaling. I mostly went to support my friend, because I really didn't think that journaling, let alone writing in a journal, was for me. She shared the techniques she had used to journal her own life starting from the time she was a little girl and how she continues today. Journaling led her to healing. She shared how her journal was a place where she could share her deepest thoughts and ask God questions.

I tried to give myself excuses by thinking that my writing needed to be neat and perfect (I am a bit OCD when it comes to that). Over and over again I heard the message, "How could you even think you could write anything meaningful?" Do I really have anything interesting to say? When am I going to find the time?" God quickly found a way for me to get past those excuses.

What excuses are holding you back from starting to journal?

_____

_____

_____

_____

When I experienced the deep, dark depression, God offered me hope and a hand. At the beginning of the hardest climb of my life out of the pit, God reminded me about journaling. I remembered Maria's teaching about healing and a place she went to share her deepest thoughts and feelings. I needed to begin to record the memories, feelings and thoughts of my past that He was revealing to me. *Psalm 147:3* *"He heals the broken hearted and binds up their wounds."* I will freely admit that it wasn't an easy process to get in the habit of writing and sharing my thoughts, because I was so good at keeping it all hidden. I was cautious to think that through writing I would heal and I couldn't have imagined how writing would become a huge part of the journey out of the brokenness.

The more time I spent journaling, the more I was able to move past writing about superficial stuff just because I felt obligated to. Soon, I was able to start freely sharing my feelings, asking tough questions, and praying for God's truth and answers. To show you what journaling has done for me, I will be sharing with you actual, personal, and intimate entries from my journal. Throughout the rest of this book, you will see journal entries that capture the good, bad and everything in between. Journaling has now become a key component in my journey to restore and transform myself into the woman that God designed me to be. *Mark 5:34* *"He said to her, "Daughter, your faith has healed you.*

Go in peace and be freed from your suffering."

Once you have made the decision to begin journaling, it takes a little bit of preparation. Consider purchasing a pretty, inspiring journal and a nice pen. Don't laugh at having a nice pen, because my obsessive, compulsiveness caused me to start journaling in pencil. I could erase the imperfections and replace it with my idea of perfection. Shortly, it became glaringly apparent that I needed to write in pen so that my imperfections could not be erased. When I had a nice pretty, inspiring journal to write in and a nice pen to write with, I was a more motivated to share my thoughts. Next, give yourself permission to share anything and everything. If there may be peering eyes or nosey people in your household, you might want to carry your journal with you, or find a secret place to safeguard it. Quite often, I carry my journal with me, because there are times when I want to record thoughts or ideas that God gives to me when I am away from home. One tip that Maria gave that day, that I know many there found very helpful and encouraging, was that not everything had to be written words. For the more creative people (which really was not me, but may be you) drawing and creating pictures to express your feelings may be a great way to journal as well.

Don't Hold Back

At first, sharing my true thoughts and feelings was really

hard; it was much easier to keep it superficial. I was afraid to go to deep into my thoughts and feelings because I wasn't sure I was quite ready to explore them. _Psalm 142:7_ _"Set me free from my prison, that I may praise your name. Then the righteous will gather about me because of your goodness to me."_ Let yourself out of your prison of hidden feelings and set yourself free.

Are you ready to explore your deepest thoughts and feelings? Why?

_____

_____

_____

_____

_____

As I gave myself permission to share and scheduled more time for journaling, I felt more comfortable expressing my thoughts and feelings. My entries moved below the surface. I didn't have to hold back anymore, because the only audience was God and me. With this revelation, I threw open the doors of my heart and held nothing back. At last, freedom was mine. _Ephesians 3:12_ _"In him and through faith in him we may approach God with freedom and confidence."_

I shared it all! At first, I yelled, got angry, complained, whined, cried, asked tough and raw questions, and told God what to do. Here are some excerpts from my journal:

> *UGH!! I don't understand why I have to go through reliving all this crap! This hurts way too much God!! Can't you just make it all go away! Why did you have to let me remember that I should have been aborted and just validate again how unwanted and unworthy I was. I hate this!!! I was happier living in my own oblivion. Now all I can see is darkness, there is not one crack of light, what are you going to do about that????????*

> *I have spent all day in bed crying my eyes out, feeling super crappy about my life. Why am I even here??????? Everyone would be so much better off without me around. I want to just die!!!! Why does this have fricken hurt so much!!!???*

As time passed, I finally had hit rock bottom, the anger was tapped out and the desperation set in.

> *Another day in bed, why can't I get out? I feel so hopeless, is there really any way out for me? I find myself in this deep, dark place, with not speck of light, what should I do? Is it time to finally just give in and end this pain? Why would I even be worth saving? Would my family even care...*

> *It has come to the time for me to decide as I can't go on*

like this anymore!! God if you are there, I am done, I am so broken and helpless. Show me a way out…

God reached out His hand to me.

Oh God, can this really be? Do you really think I am worth saving? I can start to see a ray of light in all this darkness I have been in. I actually got out of bed today and found a few moments of no tears. What is happening God? Can this last? Will I start to climb out of this deep, dark place God? Will you stay with me?

There is so much more to share and I will sprinkle excerpts throughout the remainder of this book to show just where this journey has taken me and to inspire you that there is hope in writing the journey.

Let me encourage you to not get frustrated and give up if you miss a few days or even a few weeks. When I started the journaling process, there were many times that I would miss days, because I allowed the busyness of my day to get in the way. If I had started to journal before I was ready to face this painful journey ahead, I would have given up and that would have reinforced once again my feelings of being a failure. If I miss a day or two, I tell God how sorry I am for not sharing and I pick up where I left off. Allow God to be there. Share it all and don't hold back, He wants all of you! *Psalm 25:17* "*Relieve the troubles of my heart and free me from my anguish."*

What pain and frustration might stop you from starting the journaling process?

_____

_____

_____

_____

_____

_____

_____

_____

Starting that the journaling process had me begging to ask lots of questions.

Nothing is Off Limits

I was not afraid to ask questions. In the beginning, my questions had an accusatory tone. As time passed, the tone shifted to desperation. If I were going to start to heal, I needed to be real and honest. I decided as I was learning from His Word and through the revelations of my past that I was going to challenge God with my questions of why, how, what, where and when, and any other questions that came to my mind.

What questions of why, how, what, where and when questions are you wanting to ask?

_____

_____

_____

_____

_____

I discovered that the healing process was not going to be easy or fun. I was going to have to be patient and listen--definitely not two of my greatest strengths. I was going to have to trust. My past had taught me that trusting was not a good thing to do because there was hurt right around the corner.

My Journal:

> *Okay, God, this was not a very fun day! I let myself to really get caught up in my feelings of worthlessness. Why is it that I allow myself to get caught up in the lies; they just keep circling around my head. Just when I think that I am doing good, they slip into my head. Can you show me how I can learn that when things go wrong, I don't have to automatically go back to thinking about what a loser I am and how I failed yet again?*

> *As I was reading today, God, you had me open to Daniel*

9:7 'Now, our God, hear the prayers and petitions of your servant. For your sake, Lord, look with favor on your desolate sanctuary'. I am definitely feeling desolate, Lord; are you hearing my prayers and petitions? Will you show me answers to my questions and prayers?

As I have been walking the journey, there are so many other questions that I have asked; and which He has been faithful to answer. Sometimes the answers would come right away; other times they came when I least expected them, or only when He felt the time was right. Plenty of times, when I have asked a question expecting a certain answer, He has given me a completely different answer. Sometimes He has sent me in a direction I never thought of nor could I have expected.

What are some of the questions you have been holding back asking because you are too afraid of the answers?

_____

_____

_____

_____

_____

_____

_____

All my hard-hitting and challenging questions led me to consider that maybe I should be more gracious and prayerful in my approach.

Life Support Prayer

How could I even believe that God would answer my questions or respond to my prayer requests? In the early stages, my questions were more like demands, because I so desperately wanted answers. As you go through the process of journaling, you will start to see some answers to your questions. But the answers may lead to more questions and thoughts, or they may be leading to more confusion. I have experienced both and it prompted me to start writing out my questions as prayers and thinking about in a much different way--a life support prayer. Finally, my questions went from demands to prayers. *Psalm 4:1* *"Answer me when I call to you, my righteous God. Give me relief from my distress; have mercy on me and hear my prayer."*

When my questions turned to prayers, I started off slowly. I didn't want to challenge myself too much and I thought it would make it easier for God to answer my way. Sometimes I found myself not wanting to pray for anything good to happen, because I was afraid of being disappointed. I feared that He would not answer, because I wasn't worthy enough of His love and grace. *Job 9:16* *(TLB) "And even if my prayers were answered, I could scarce believe that he had heard my cry.*

What prayers might you be holding back because you don't feel you deserve to ask them?

_____

_____

_____

_____

_____

_____

God has been so faithful to answer the prayers that He knew would lead me on the path towards my purpose. It has not always been what I expected, but it was what I needed.

When we start to let go of the fear, doubt and nervous feelings about praying for ourselves, that is when God can begin His work in us. The good work He has for us will not always be easy. In fact, it may be downright hard and painful. Oh, have I learned this from personal experience. I share throughout this book some really hard work I had to do. The lessons, hope, and encouragement I received made the painful journey well worth walking through.

My Journal:

> *... Lord thank you for letting me know that I have value. After meeting with a client today, I felt like I was truly able to help her begin to see herself in a different light. Lord, I pray that you would begin to show me how I can turn that feeling towards myself. I still see that "woman" staring back at me. I pray that you could show me ways to do a better job of shifting my perspective even more. That feeling I had today, could you begin to show me that I can see myself in a whole new light?*

As we start to move into a deeper understanding of who God is moving us to become, the prayers get more focused, specific, and personal. We begin to moving past the pain and start the journey to grow and receive better understanding. In this place, God can give us the knowledge, hope, encouragement we need to keep pressing through. Other areas will begin to surface and you will need to address them by starting the whole process over again.

My Journal:

> *...Lord I am starting to see the bigger picture. You are calling me to share my message and that is a little scary. You're wanting me to speak to women, to encourage and inspire them in the hope you have for them. I pray, God,*

that you guide me in the direction I am to share, that you will show me the best way for them to receive the message, and that I can remain confident enough to share the most vulnerable parts of my journey.

Although writing out my questions and prayers has been an important part of my journey, I also have conversations with God. Those conversations can be a little lopsided with me doing all the talking. But when I finally stop talking and sharing, and began to sit still and listen, I received some of my best insights, knowledge, inspiration and even answers I wasn't expecting. It's in these times of listening that journaling has taught me valuable lessons and I experienced the greatest growth.

Let me encourage you not to allow your prayers to go unasked; you will never know how amazing things could be or what God has in store unless you ask. Make written and conversational prayer a big part of your journey. *Colossians 4:2* *"Devote yourselves to prayer, being watchful and thankful."*

Another step, in the journey to becoming the woman He predestined you to be, is committing to begin the healing process. The most valuable tool for me in this process was journaling. Surrendering our areas of brokenness and allowing ourselves to heal are vital steps in the restoration process. Don't allow your excuses to stop you from taking this very important step. The freedom that God gives you will far surpass anything you could have ever imagined.

Don't hold back your emotions; express them freely while you are journaling. There were many times in the beginning when I felt a sense of relief after I was done writing and sharing that day. I have only shared bits and pieces of the feelings I had, but it was an important step for me to take. As I was preparing to write this book, I re-read journal entries from the recent past. I am so grateful that I am no longer the broken, shattered woman who began this journey. I am still a work-in-progress and He is still hard at work on me. _Philippians 1:6_ (TLB) "And I am sure that God who began the good work within you will keep right on helping you grow in his grace until his task within you is finally finished on the day when Jesus Christ returns."

Asking God questions and seeing how He answered them gave me a peace of mind; the practice became such a key component of the restoration process. I have learned that God does not cause bad things to happen to us. He created us all with free will and there are consequences that come with the choices we make. Likewise, the people who hurt us may have been acting out of their own pain; their bad choices resulted in our hurts. I am far from perfect and my words and actions have hurt others, but through prayer God was able to show me how to change and how to heal.

Writing my prayers and conversing with God has sustained me through this journey. He was the one person who would listen and not to try to fix me. He let me-be-me, then He guided me through answers to my questions and my conversations with Him. I have grown so much in the prayer process and I am still learning and growing. Later, I will share more about learning to pray beyond possibilities.

If your healing journey doesn't include journaling, I pray that you will find an outlet in which you can express yourself freely and ask questions. Always take it to Him in prayer.

Expressing yourself through prayer will build the strength you will need for the journey that lies ahead in finding your true worth.

Spending 45 years of my life in broken, shattered pieces left me hopeless and struggling to find any worth or value in my life. But I am on a journey in which God is restoring me. He has given me hope and showed me how worthy and valuable I really am. _Matthew 10:29-31_ (MSG) "What's the price of a pet canary? Some loose change, right? And God cares what happens to it even more than you do. He pays even great attention to you, down to the last detail – even numbering the hairs on your head! So don't be intimidated by all this bully talk. You are worth more than a *million canaries."*

The next big step as I climbed out of the pit was discovering and accepting that I actually had value and worth.

3 Finding Worth in the Worthlessness

When you are staring at a full pill bottle deciding whether or not your life is worth living, that last thing you are thinking about is finding your worth and value. Everything around you feels hopeless, dark, and depressing. As I have shared, that was my crossroads. I had a life or death choice to make; I gave God one last opportunity to show me that He thought I was worth saving. God answered my challenge by blessing me with a sliver of light, a hint of hope, and sense of value that I had never experienced before.

After a lifetime of feeling unworthy and worthless, you can find yourself at the bottom of a deep, dark pit. Climbing out will be one of the most daunting and difficult tasks you will ever undertake. Looking up from the bottom of the pit, the climb looks ominous and overwhelming. I know all too well the paralyzing fear nearly stopped me from making the climb. Just taking that first step to find worth in your feelings of worthless-ness can be challenging. Make an investment in yourself and your future--take this first step. It is the hardest one, but it can be one of the most important, rewarding steps you will experience. It was exactly what I had to do. The next step didn't take me quite as long to make. It was still really hard, but each step up the mountain gets a little easier and a little less painful.

After taking those first couple of what seems–like-impossible steps, the journey up the mountain has begun. Along the way, there will be times where you reach a plateau; God is parking us there to do a little, or in my case a lot of, extra work. There have been a couple of times when I have slipped and tumbled back down the mountain, too. I got stuck one or two times, okay more, in the deep cracks of brokenness, yet the lessons I was learning along the climb motivated me to pick myself back up and continue the arduous climb.

Finding my worth was my first big, daunting step. I had to take a long, hard look at the woman staring back at me in the mirror and ask myself what I was allowing to define my self-image. My next step was to rediscover my value and redefine my worth, not by what I thought or had been told, but by God's word.

There are lots of steps still left to take, but I am taking them with God on and by my side.

Do you have any daunting steps ahead of you to find out who you were created to be?

_____

_____

_____

_____

This is What I See

Images flash before our eyes constantly bombarding us with the world's view of beauty and beautiful. From the pages of *Sports Illustrated Swimsuit Issue* to every other fashion magazine, from the movies to reality TV. Magazines at the grocery store checkout tell us "How to Look Younger", "How to Lose 20 lbs. in 10 Days", "How to be Sexier to Hold onto Your Man", and they share"101 Beauty Secrets".

How do you think the media is trying to shape your definition of personal beauty?

_____

_____

_____

_____

_____

The messages for years were telling me that I needed to be perfect--be the perfect weight, wear the perfect clothes, have long beautiful hair and makeup just like the cover model. As I got up every morning and I looked in the mirror, I realized that I was not the perfect weight, my clothes were average, my hair was short and graying, and I was nowhere close to looking like a cover model. My mirror started to crack under the pressure of the world's view, and over the years the cracks got bigger and deeper.

The media keeps us wanting and striving for what is not meant for us. _1 John 4:5_ *"They are from the world and therefore speak from the viewpoint of the world, and the world listens to them."* This is how the enemy works, He wants us to keep listening to what the world says about how we should look. But we don't have to listen to the world anymore.

My Journal:

> *God, why is it that I am at a healthy, normal weight for what medical doctors say, yet all I can see it that 253 pound woman I used to be years ago? I just don't understand... I should be happy!!! I don't use food anymore to hide my pain, but why do I still hurt? I should feel happier, thinner, prettier, more valuable and more worth. Why don't I??? Please, Lord, show me what I so desperately need! How to find out who I really am; what I*

was created to do and why I am special to you?! I am begging here on my knees ready, Lord, to be better; I am so tired of the darkness. I am climbing the mountain; keep me climbing, don't allow my feet to slip back. Keep my vision focused on you and not what I trick my eyes into seeing.

Another entry:

Oh Lord, why is it that I can't see myself the way I know you see me? Why is it that I can't see myself the way my hubby sees me? He tells me every day how sexy and beautiful I am, but I can't accept it. I always find a way to blow him off or put myself down. I deny him and tell him his vision is wrong, and I also deny Your vision of me. Please open my eyes and my heart, Lord, that I can see the real me-- what you created this woman for and who I was meant to be so long ago. Allow me to see the little girl who felt pretty before the world and people told her differently.

Why is it that we allow the media, print, film or TV to influence how we look at ourselves?

Does your negative self-talk deepen the cracks in your mirror? Why?

_____

_____

What are you telling yourself every day when you look in your mirror?

_____

_____

_____

_____

_____

_____

As a society, we measure people's value and worth by their beauty and confidence. We allow the marketing companies and social media to define beauty and what we should look like. To boost our self-worth we post our lives on social media so that others can see our amazing and fabulous lives. But the truth is that our society is so desperately broken. Most of us are not willing to share our flaws and weakness, because we fear what people might think. Don't get me wrong, there are plenty of times where what we share are truly great things happening in our lives, but there is so much more to us than what we show.

Not long ago as I looked at myself in the mirror, I truly felt like there was no purpose for my existence. I didn't think there was really anything good about me. My distorted self-image told me I was not pretty, not smart, not worthy; I had nothing to offer, and I was good for nothing. The rocks keep flying with every word and the cracks in my mirror got deeper and longer.

There are millions of secular self-help books, which focus on self-image and how others view us. The subtitle of this book is *A Journey to Restore a Shattered Self-Image*. Honestly, when this journey started, it was all about ME. How could I see myself better? How could I feel better about myself? How could I get people to like me?

My Journal:

> *I am so tired of seeing this 253 lb. woman in the mirror. For years I have been the way I am now; I am healthy and alive. I want to see myself as a beautiful, confident woman. Will that ever happen???? If I could just feel better about myself, God, then I could actually start to feel like I mattered and that I could open myself to people. I want to be myself, whatever that is!?*

I was so focused on myself, I didn't understand how selfish that really was. God quickly showed me in <u>*Deuteronomy 4:16*</u> *"so that you do not become corrupt and make for yourselves an idol, an image of any shape, whether formed like a man or a woman."* I had become my own idol in the way I looked and thought about myself. OUCH!

I was building an idol to myself and what I wanted and I

needed. Isn't that where most of us have to start? The desire to make a change and sacrifice ourselves to God is the first step to restoring our God-created image which has been damaged by all the hurt, pain, anger, and the circumstances in our lives. I had to surrender my selfishness to God and He was able to show me the reason for which I was created.

My Journal:

> *God, why do I see myself this way? Why can't I accept this woman I see standing here? All I can see is a girl who felt unwanted, who never measured up to anyone's standards or expectations. I see an ugly duckling who never quite fit in with her peers, who tried so hard but just failed over and over again. You revealed something to me today in Psalm 139:14-18, "I praise you because I am fearfully and wonderfully made; your works are wonderful, I know that full well. My frame was not hidden from you when I was made in the secret place, when I was woven together in the depths of the earth. Your eyes saw my unformed body; all the days ordained for me were written in your book before one of them came to be. How precious to me are your thoughts, God! How vast is the sum of them! Were I to count them, they would outnumber the grains of sand— when I awake, I am still with you." If this is true, Lord, help*

me see myself through your eyes, if I am created for a specific purpose, what is it and why do I have to feel this pain?

Another entry:

Ok, God, things are starting to make sense, it been a few months and I am realizing that I am a bit thick headed (lol). I can start to see why I went through all the hurt and pain. It still really sucks, God, going through all this stuff: felling unaccepted, feeling unwanted, feeling like a complete failure, not feeling smart enough, and all the other stupid things I have thought about myself. You are showing me that I am not those things; but it is still hard to believe. You know it takes a while for things to sink in. After 44 years of believing the lies about myself, I'm starting to believe in who you created me to be.

We also live in a world where we judge a book by its cover. Even though, as kids and as Christians, we are taught not to, it is in our flawed human natures to judge. We make instant assessments of people based on their physical appearance, how they talk, what they say, and how they dress. I am so guilty of doing this!

When you meet someone for the first time, what is your basis for judging them?

_____

_____

_____

On what basis would you want someone to judge you?

_____

_____

_____

When I worked as a stylist, it was my job to judge a "book by its cover", and see how I could make it more beautiful and presentable to the world. However, here is what my clients learned about me: I was not a stylist whose only goal was to make the outside shine nice and pretty to meet the world's view of beauty. I encouraged women to allow their inner beauty to shine so brightly that their outside appearance was an expression of who they truly were inside. Yet, I still reached a point in my career when I was stagnating; it was hard to get motivated. I struggled to figure out the reason for my lack of enthusiasm. I asked God to help me reignite my passion to encourage and inspire women, but He had another plan for me...

My Journal:

> *Okay God, that was an eye opening day! I was sitting in my office arranging my client folders on my computer and you have stopped me in my tracks... what do you mean I need to make myself my client? That I needed to dress the part!!! What are you trying to say??????*

Another entry:

> *What do you mean I need to see the real inner beauty in me? Yes, I encourage women to see and break through their negative opinions of themselves, to accept the beauty and bodies just as they are now. Okay, that was a V8 moment, Lord. You want me to start getting rid of all the negative talk and feelings that I have for myself. I am not sure I am up to that task, God. It is so much easier to see it in others, but you want me to look at myself that way?! Is that really possible God? I am really ready to do that kinda work on me. Would I really hire me right now? Are you sure God?*

God had given me the assignment. I started the work of changing my view of myself, and not judging myself by the world's standards. I learned not to let the negative self-talk or the things others had said stop me from seeing myself through His eyes. I struggle from time-to-time with allowing that old version and thoughts of myself to creep back in. I continue on my journey and I see Him at work on me; He has given me a purpose, an assignment that exposes my weaknesses and my struggles.

Is God giving you an assignment you should be working on? What is it?

_____

_____

_____

_____

_____

As women, not only are we influenced by the world's view of beauty, but we compare ourselves to the women whom the world views as beautiful. How do we measure up? When we base our value and worth on the world's standards and compare ourselves to others, we get a distorted picture of ourselves.

God Thinks I'm What...

My mom thought that I was not worth keeping, and through emotional distance she continued to show her disappointment in me throughout my childhood. When I found myself searching for someone to find me worthy enough to love and to value me for who I was, it led to a lot of negative thoughts, sadness and loneliness.

Every time I looked in my mirror, it told me that I was unworthy, not good enough to deserve something or someone to love me. It told me that no one would see the good in me or respect me. I grew up in a home with a mom and dad, but I never truly felt wanted or deeply loved by my mother. My dad was the only one who ever truly showed interest in me and in what I was doing; yet I still felt like I never measured up. The feeling of being worthless began when I was very young and continued as I grew up; I didn't realize its long-lasting impact until I found myself in that deep, dark pit of depression as an adult.

My Journal:

> *Dear God, things have been really hard lately! I am finding it really hard to find any reasons that I should still be here. I know how much I would hurt my family, so I guess that is why I chose to not just end it all. This morning started like every other morning. All I could see was a woman who was unworthy of love, a complete failure as a mom, wife and person, what could I possibly offer the world today? As I stood there after getting my makeup on, the tears started to flow (that really hadn't happened too much before God). Why did you make me worth saving? Why, God, do I feel like a complete waste of space? Why couldn't my life be different? Surely there have to be people more worthy*

of your love and time...

I had to open my mind and heart to really search God's Word to discover why I was so worthy of His love and why He valued me so much. My foundation was contained in the words of *Psalm 139:13-16* *"For you created my inmost being; you knit me together in my mother's womb. I praise you because I am fearfully and wonderfully made; your works are wonderful, I know that full well. My frame was not hidden from you when I was made in the secret place, when I was woven together in the depths of the earth. Your eyes saw my unformed body; all the days ordained for me were written in your book before one of them came to be."* I needed to start picking up the shattered, broken pieces that led to my feelings of unworthiness. In *Psalm 119:37 (NLT)* the Psalmist wrote these words *"Turn my eyes from worthless things, and give me life through your word."* In my desperate and broken state, this spoke profoundly to me. He was counseling me to turn my eyes away from all those feelings of worthlessness and accept the life He had given me through His Word. Of course, I needed more encouragement, and I still need validation and reassurance today.

In studying the Apostle Paul's letter to the Philippian church, I found the answers I was seeking. *Philippians 3:8 (AMP)* *"Yes, furthermore, I count everything as loss compared to the possession of the priceless privilege (the overwhelming preciousness, the surpassing worth, and supreme advantage) of knowing Christ Jesus my Lord and of progressively becoming more deeply and intimately acquainted with Him [of perceiving and recognizing and understanding Him more fully and clearly]. For His sake I have lost everything and consider it all to be mere rubbish (refuse, dregs), in order that I may win (gain) Christ (the Anointed One)."* We get the priceless privilege, surpassing our worth and knowledge, of knowing Jesus more deeply and intimately, recognizing and understanding Him more clearly. I will gladly surrender what I have discovered about my brokenness to Him to know Him in that way!

Can you begin to believe you are worthy? Why?

_____

_____

_____

_____

_____

Finding my value to Him was my next challenge to overcome. Growing up having failed in every attempt I made to gain approval, I learned what my true value was--*nothing*. To learn about God's perspective on worth and value, I turned to His Word. God has given many examples of people he found valuable, and I have always been in awe of the value He placed on David.

One particular situation stood out to me. In 1 Samuel when David and King Saul are having a conversation, and the king admits how foolish he has been and he assures David that he would not try to harm him again. In _1 Samuel 26:23-24_ David's words are recorded, *"The LORD rewards everyone for their righteousness and faithfulness. The LORD delivered you into my hands today, but I would not lay a hand on the LORD's anointed. As surely as I valued your life today, so may the LORD value my life and deliver me from all trouble."* Like David, our life is very valuable to God and He wants to deliver us from all our troubles; we have everlasting life because Jesus, His son, died for all our troubles.

We are so valuable to Him that He numbers the hairs on our heads; as it says in _Luke 12:7a (AMP),_ *"But [even] the very hairs of your head are all numbered..."* This was hard for me to fathom at first; just like all the other scriptures that point out how worthy and valuable I am to Him. Yet, as I am developing a deeper and more intimate relationship with Him, I am finding a new definition of my worth and value. Our value and worth can only be found in His significance in our lives.

Can you begin to believe you are valuable? Why?

_____

_____

_____

Where Does this Journey Lead?

If you are anything like me, you probably don't think that you deserve nor are you even capable of having a life of worth, significance, or meaning. I spent decades feeling that way. Whether it is circumstances or people have hurt us and held us back or our own negative self-talk, we have become numb to the fact we can or deserve to feel significant, like we matter.

What are the reasons you feel you don't deserve a life of significance or feeling like you matter?

_____

_____

_____

_____

_____

_____

_____

_____

I had let my feelings and negative self-talk determine who I was and what I was worth. I held myself back from experiencing the significance and meaning that God had for me. I had wasted so many years caught up in the lies that I let others tell me, and what I choose to believe about myself.

What is holding you back for experiencing a life of significance and meaning?

_____

_____

_____

_____

_____

_____

I wish I could tell you that I flipped a switch and I was immediately healed of all my fears, doubts and degrading self-talk; that has not been the case. There are many times that I still beat myself up for wasting so much time being lost in the my own little world. God is amazing and I believe wholeheartedly that there can be an instantaneous healing; it was just not His plan for me. I have had to make that journey up the steep mountain, taking lots of steps forward and slipping a few steps back, to discover the true significance and meaning God had for me and my life.

I can tell you and reassure you of this: He has a life of significance and meaning for each and every one of us. Look at the examples of what Jesus did for some of the most broken women He encountered. The Samaritan woman, *(John 4:7-30)* who spoke with Jesus, was shocked that He knew her every sin and saw all her brokenness. He saw past all negatives to see the real, beautiful woman she was. The woman who was bleeding from everywhere on her body (*Matthew 9:20-22*) had been outcast; desperately she reached out to Jesus for physical healing, and she was instantly healed and restored. The crippled woman's distorted body (*Luke 13:10-13*) Jesus healed and restored. The common theme in these three women's stories was that they all had physical and emotional ailments. They all had hurt, pain, and broken pieces of their lives that need to be healed and restored.

Can you relate to any of these women? Do you have a negative and shameful view of who you are? Are you just so tired of bleeding out with pain and anger, or does your distorted image of your body and who you are dominate your life? I have at different points of my life; in the deep, dark pit, they all converged. There is hope, restoration and healing meant for you, and it can be found in God.

Only God can give us the life of significance and meaning that we are truly and desperately seek. Not only because we are so very worth it to him, but because He also gave us a promise. In *Jeremiah 29:11* "*For I know the plans I have for you, declares the Lord, plans to prosper you and not to harm you, plans to give you hope and a future.*" He has a plan, He has a purpose for us, and He will gives us hope and a future. The promise gets better and even more exciting in verses _12-14a_, *"Then you will call on me and come and pray to me, and I will listen to you. You will seek me and find me when you seek me with all your heart. I will be found by you, declares the Lord, and will bring you back from captivity."* These verses became an important reminder that when we come to Him in prayer, He is there. When we go looking for Him in our hearts, He is there. Being held captive by our feelings of worthlessness, He is there to release us. I find these verses so exciting! There is so much hope in these promises, in His purpose of hope, and the future for us.

My journey from worthless to worthy has been long and painful; but the transformation is nothing short of miraculous. When I look in the mirror now, I no longer see the 253-pound woman who was eating herself to death, while thinking she was ugly, unintelligent, and worthless. Instead, I see myself as a beautiful, wonderfully made woman who has many gifts and talents (which I have just have begun to discover). I am fully convinced that I am created in His image. It is okay to call ourselves beautiful; we are speaking the truth of God's Word. The world tells us that it is conceited, self-righteous, and haughty if we even start to even think we are beautiful. Everything about God is beautiful, graceful, merciful and meaningful, and so are we.

I challenged myself to fully dive into God's Word to

discover why I was worthy and valuable enough for Him to save me. I returned again to *Psalms 139:13-16* which told me how God was intimately acquainted with me before I was even born. Reading these verses early in my journey impacted me profoundly; I understood how truly valuable and worthy I was to Him. Having lived my life feeling like I was unwanted, knowing I should have been aborted, and even contemplating why I should even be here, my eyes and heart were opened to God laying my path out before me.

Gaining a new vision of my God-created image and believing how God's sees me has set me free from the captivity of my distorted self-image. Discovering I was worthy of His unconditional love, grace, mercy and forgiveness and learning that my life had value to Him, have led me to embrace the significance and meaning that He had intended for me along.

Staying grounded in His Word, being honest and transparent in our prayers and accepting His vision of us, we can find a transformed image. Discovering our worth and our value to Him lead us to His abundant significance for our lives and inspires us to impact others.

I have begun walking on His path, I have written my personal, intimate thoughts and conversations with God in my journal. He has taken me from the depths of darkness, and has guided me on my climb out of the deep pit, so that you will believe that there is HOPE, I want to share with you some of those thoughts and conversations I shared with God. I want to inspire you to believe that there is so much hope out there for YOU. Discovering my true self came through many tears, lots of questions, and tons of journaling. Believing His vision of me has begun to transform me into a woman who is confident in my beauty, my purpose, my value, my worth and my significance as His daughter. Created to be special, unique, and beautiful.

This broken and shattered little girl is leaving behind the unworthiness and hurt. I am seeking the restoration and transformation that will reveal me as His wonderful and beautiful creation. Through God, I am worthy of love, worthy of feeling like I matter, and worthy to impact the lives of other women who have experienced these same feelings.

Even after all of this progress, a few more complicated and daunting steps were ahead. I had to face the voices running around in my head.

4 Living with the Voices

Riley is a happy, 11-year-old, mid-western girl, whose world gets turn upside down. Her emotions try to guide her through a difficult life-changing event; however, the stress brings one particular emotion to the forefront. If you have children who like Disney movies, or are willing to admit you like Disney movies, then you'll realize this is a paraphrase of the plot for the movie "Inside Out". Riley's emotions, the voices in her head, were joy, fear, sadness, disgust and anger. I wish that those were the only voices that existed in my head. During my darkest days fear, sadness, and anger were the voices that shouted the loudest.

What voices are running around in your head?

_____

_____

_____

I also lived with these voices: shame, regret, failure, doubt, hurt, unworthiness, unforgiveness, and comparison. But my biggest struggles have been with fear, doubt, rejection, comparison and perfectionism.

Fear paralyzed me, especially the fear of failure. My fear was so all consuming that I became frozen. All my fears were like ice in my heart and kept me from moving forward, backward or sideways. I was so afraid that one mistake or wrong move would destroy me.

Doubt and rejection left me questioning everything: my value, my worth, and my hope. Doubt, like fear, stopped me in my tracks; I was always wondering, "What if...?" Rejection was lurking right around the corner, ready to prove that my worst doubts were true.

Comparison and perfectionism kept me very dissatisfied. When I looked at people, I saw those whom I thought were prettier, more worthy, and more successful than me. Why couldn't I be more like them or like my husband who is smart, witty, and fearless? Why couldn't I be as loving and gracious as other moms were with their children? Over and over I repeated the phrase, "Why couldn't I be more like..."; this kept me stuck comparing and trying to be perfect.

_Forget _Everything _And _Run

I had spent a lifetime trying to out-run my fears, that I did not realize they had already devoured me. It was a dreadful moment when I discovered that I had lived with overwhelming, debilitating and paralyzing fear. Here was my "AHA!", God-given moment of perspective:

Excerpt from my Blog:

> *I learned a great lesson while at Daily Disciples women's retreat. As part of our Saturday night session, the room of about 50 women were split up; half on one wall, half on the other. The speakers began to ask some pretty tough questions and if our answers were yes, we were to walk into the middle of the room. There were questions like "Have you battled depression?", "Have you had an abortion?", and many other very tough questions. Although the questions were hard and painful, we were encouraged to be transparent and honest. We looked into the eyes of other women who had experienced the same things we had: guilt, shame, and condemnation for our actions or for what we thought we had done wrong. I met plenty of women in the middle of the room."*
>
> *The question that left me shaken to my core was: "Have you experienced fear?" On the surface that is a pretty mild question and 99% of the women walked to the*

middle, but it was what happened next that brought me to my knees and tears later that night. "Who deals with debilitating fear?" I decided for once in my life I would stay, instead of running away. I could look to see other women standing there, others who knew and understood what I was struggling with. Yet one by one they walked back to their sides, and one person was left standing there all alone--me. Scared to death by what that meant, standing there putting on my brave and steady mask, I shook it off like it was no big deal.

Could I have really been the only one who dealt with fear that paralyzed her life for decades? Fear of failure, fear of disappointing others, fear of being loved, fear of being worthy, and fear of feeling wanted. God, why only me, was my question. Later that night during prayer and worship time I fell to my knees, tears streaming down my face, mascara smeared everywhere, and the Lord spoke to me with a clarity that I have never experienced before. "My daughter, those with the greatest fears will be experience the greatest faith and celebrate the greatest victories." Once we were back in the room, I cleaned myself up and I wrote in my journal.

Dear God, I can't believe the moment we shared tonight, I have never heard you speak so clearly to me. I truly can't believe what you said to me; I am still in awe and shock of that moment. WOW, you showed me a love and peace that I never have felt. It felt like you were right there sitting next to me with your arm around me, whispering in my ear. Even with all the fears, I can still have the chance to experience great faith? Am I really deserving of that honor? I can celebrate the victories that come along with faith? I have never celebrated any of my successes. I am at a loss right now, Lord, and I am turning it all over to you. I lay my life at your feet; I am open to what is next...

Little did I know how big and life changing that statement, "I am open to what is next," really was. That was His invitation to open the doors to what would become my purpose and passion.

God's plan and purpose for our lives are so much greater than we could ever imagine. We need to be reminded, as His daughters that our faith will be greater and our victories will be sweeter because we are choosing to let go of our fear and leave it at the foot of His cross. The cross that Jesus died on so that we may receive all the grace, mercy, forgiveness, and unconditional love that He has to give and offer us. I'm sure that I will experience fear again and again, but I know that I can lay those fears again at His feet. You, too, can lay all your burdens, pain, grief, doubt, disappointment, and fear that paralyze your life at foot of His cross; and His grace and unconditional love will cover it all.

What fears are you willing to let go?

_____

_____

_____

_____

_____

Will you lay all your fears at the foot of His cross? Why?

_____

_____

_____

_____

_____

After my overwhelming moment of clarity and under-standing, it was time to look at all my fears, to define what they were and how I could overcome them. Did you notice that I said *define* and not *get rid of*? When seeking to define my fears, what was brought to the surface were some very big and overwhelming thoughts. Why? Because it has taken years for the cracks to become really deep and turn into paralyzing fears. There was one really big, scary fear to face: fear of failure. While there are quite a few other fears, I knew that I had to take a good hard look at the "Big One" first.

Do you have a fear of failure? Why?

_____

_____

_____

_____

_____

That fearful thought of failure is what truly brought me to my knees that night at the retreat. Failure to meet others expectations. Failure by disappointing others with my imperfections. Failure to believe that I could possibly be worth anything good. My failure was all based on past performance and the doubt of ever performing up to the expectations of others.

My Journal:

God, why is it that I think I have to be perfect in every way? I have always based my success on how I performed. I seemed to always fail in my performance. I was supposed to do well in school, I needed to live up to my potential, but I failed. Even my best efforts weren't good enough. I tried and tried to get my mom to like me, but I failed. My vision of performance, whether I thought I did good or bad, was never enough—failed again. Help me see a way not to judge myself based on what everyone thinks is top performance; instead show me what living a life for you represents.

Another entry:

> Today, God, I finally got a glimpse of how much more important it is to act honorably than it is to perform for the world. I had to have open eyes and heart today God, to see a hurting woman at the mall. Instead of walking by her (which would have been what the world would have done), I stopped and asked her if she was ok. That was WAY out of my comfort zone, Lord, yet she shared with me her pain and I shared with her my story. I asked her if I could pray with and for her, and I did. It was so overwhelming to know that this was not a performance for the world, but rather a time that I was pursuing Your will. It was so overwhelming, God, to watch as her pain (even if for just a moment) fade away and she left with a smile. That is - success; thank you for finally getting that lesson through my thick skull. It takes me a while, Lord, as you know, but I am thankful for your patience and grace.

<u>Psalm 38:17-19</u> *"I'm on the edge of losing it— the pain in my gut keeps burning. I'm ready to tell my story of failure; I'm no longer smug in my sin."* These verses described exactly how I was feeling as I was discovering the depths of my fear and what it was going to take to overcome it. I had no idea what God had in store me, but I could whole-heartily say, I'm ready to tell my story of failure; I am no longer smug in my sin. God's life-changing plan for

me included Him telling me that I was going to write this book. Ahhhhh! God, you want me to do WHAT? At that point He had prepared me to tell my story, but I was not ready to write or speak about it. The thought of having to write it down brought on a whole new set of fears and anxiety. Acknowledged and overcome (well sort of).

The verse that began to free me from letting my failure define me was *Psalm 32:5* which reads, *"Then I let it all out; I said, I'll make a clean breast of my failures to GOD. Suddenly the pressure was gone—my guilt dissolved, my sin disappeared."* When I finally surrendered all that fear of failure, I actually did feel the pressure was removed; my guilt and shame were wiped clean. My struggle in this area is not over and I go back to this verse quite frequently.

There are many reasons we face failure. Often we simply make honest mistakes. Sometimes we are not prepared or gifted to tackle a particular challenge. But, sadly, other times, we sabotage our own efforts by allowing negative self-talk about our past failures keep us from success in the present.

Thankfully, there is hope for those of us who battle this fear. Through an intimate relationship with Christ, we can overcome the fear of failure and really any other fear we may have. But, overcoming this fear doesn't mean perfection. It means that we are becoming better equipped to deal with the future mistakes and failures, quicker to find the lessons and gifts, as well as being more forgiving with ourselves. A famous Thomas Edison quotation reads, *"I have not failed. I've just found 10,000 ways that won't work."* When we keep trying, we are not failing; the only way we can fail is to quit trying.

Are you willing to keep trying even it takes 10,000 times that don't work? Why?

_____

_____

_____

_____

_____

Doubt Steals, Rejection Kills

Doubt and rejection were very slippery steps on the climb out of that deep dark pit I had landed in. Doubt was stealing my life and rejection was killing my hope. I experienced doubt in two ways: first, doubt in myself and my abilities, and second, doubt at times in my faith. My self-doubt came in the form of an accusing voice on an endless loop asking, "Why would you ever think you could be good enough or even special?" Listening to that obnoxious voice, that shouted at me in every opportunity or decision, prevented me from realizing how much I was holding myself back. Every time I allowed myself to let doubt steal from me, I turned back to His Word and referred to *Luke 24:38 (NLT)* *"Why are you frightened? he asked. Why are your hearts filled with doubt?"* I speak to my self-doubt by asking myself those two questions: "Why am I afraid" and "Why am I really doubting?" I can step back and be more objective to distinguish what is the truth and what is a lie. By studying and applying God's Word every time, knowing that He is on my side, and sensing Him here with me, I can overcome that voice of doubt.

When I entertained doubts about myself, I started to feel like rejection was hiding around every corner. If I were not good enough, then no one would want to be around me. I would be alone and rejected. My mother couldn't even love me; she rejected me. I projected that rejection onto everyone else and I expected them to reject me as well. To avoid feeling rejected, I hid myself away in my own little world within the walls of my home. I ventured out only when it was absolutely necessary for my family.

For me to overcome the voices of doubt and rejection, I had to be willing to take risks and step out on faith. I will admit that, at first, I would only let my toe go over the edge of the step. Once I found that it was safe, I began to take slightly larger steps. Studying and believing God's Word strengthened my faith. The stronger my faith grew, the softer the voices of self-doubt became and the thoughts of rejection subsided. What God thinks of me is more important that what others think of me. He does not doubt who He created me to be and He will never reject me. Don't beat yourself up if you give in to the feelings of doubt and rejection. I continue to struggle with them myself; yet He will always bring me back to Him. My doubt He will turn into joy and my fear of rejection He will replace with hope.

How are doubt and the fear of rejection holding you back?

_____

_____

_____

_____

_____

What is it costing you?

_____

_____

_____

_____

Now that I have turned down the volume on voices of doubt and rejection, I had to get to work on the other voices-- comparison and perfection.

Must Measure Up

Do you ever compare yourself to others? I know that I spent my entire life doing it and it has been very unfulfilling. When I concentrate on the beauty, talents, and gifts that God has given others, I fail to appreciate what He has given me.

There are two ways to look at comparison. First, we can look at things to see how they are similar or different. Secondly, we can observe if two or more things are similar or in the same category. What I find interesting is that there is no mention that the items being compared have to be an exact match. I had a distorted view of comparison in which I compared my imperfect self with what I thought was perfect about the other people. In every case, I fell short. The quicksand of comparison can devour you before you even know what has happened.

What areas do you compare yourself to others? Why?

_____

_____

_____

_____

_____

_____

_____

Consider this verse in _Lamentations 2:13_ (TLB) _"In all the world has there ever been such sorrow? O Jerusalem, what can I compare your anguish to? How can I comfort you? For your wound is deep as the sea. Who can heal you?"_ If we think about ourselves as Jerusalem, what would our answers be to these questions: In all the world has there ever been such sorrow? **What is your sorrow?**

_____

_____

_____

_____

What can I compare your anguish to? **_Does your anguish really compare to others? Why?_**

_____

_____

_____

_____

God wants us to know that He can comfort us. He knows we have been deeply wounded. How can God comfort you? **_Do you realize who can heal you and why?_**

_____

_____

_____

_____

When I asked myself these questions, the answers revealed how deeply wounded I was. The young girl, who compared herself to her peers, never felt she was ever good enough. The adolescent thought she wasn't as likeable as everyone else. The adult compared her imperfection to everyone else's perfection and came up lacking. Even now as I write this, I am comparing my anguish to that of victims of abuse or other horrific acts, and I am nearly invalidating my own pain. But God doesn't compare our anguish, heartache or wounds to those of others.

For a long time, I didn't feel that God could comfort me. Why He would even want to comfort me? I surely didn't think He could heal me, because I was just too broken and damaged. Yet He has been faithful to this broken, shattered girl. He wants for each on us to know that He will comfort us and restore all of shattered, jagged pieces of our life. He will put us back together, piece by piece, one by one.

I really love how the Apostle Paul writes in *2 Corinthians 10:12* (TLB) *"Oh, don't worry, I wouldn't dare say that I am as wonderful as these other men who tell you how good they are! Their trouble is that they are only comparing themselves with each other and measuring themselves against their own little ideas. What stupidity!"* Can we adopt this attitude in our daily lives? If so, what would that look like? Let's not get caught up in comparing ourselves to those who boast and think so highly of themselves. Let's compare ourselves to God's Word and live out what He has called us to do.

How are you impacted by what Paul says here about comparing ourselves to others?

_____

_____

_____

_____

_____

My Journal:

> *Oh Lord, how can I stop comparing myself with others. Why do I feel I have to measure up to those who have the gifts and talents are different than mine? Why can't I see what my gifts and talents are? Do I even have any? Open my eyes, Lord, to see what you see in me. Show me what special gifts and talents that you have given me.*

How easy it is to become caught up in the world's view of what is ideal. We live in a world that continuously streams images of what beauty is and what it should look like. We truly never get a break from it; it runs 24/7 all over the world. The message is that we should conform to their version of beautiful.

For most of my life, I struggled to meet the expectations of society and the world. Liked and accepted, pretty and thin, smart and capable. My early failures and negative self-talk convinced me that all of it was beyond my reach. *Romans 6:16 (AMP)* teaches us, *"Do you not know that if you continually surrender yourselves to anyone to do His will, you are the slaves of him whom you obey, whether that be to sin, which leads to death, or to obedience which leads to righteousness (right doing and right standing with God)?"* By surrendering myself to negativity, I became the slave to my insufficiency.

God has provided a way for us to be set free from negative self-talk and societal expectations. The Apostle Paul reveals that our freedom is found in having our minds renewed by God. In *Romans 12:2 (AMP)*, he writes, *"Do not be conformed to this world (this age), [fashioned after and adapted to its external, superficial customs], but be transformed (changed) by the [entire] renewal of your mind [by its new ideals and its new attitude], so that you may prove [for yourselves] what is the good and acceptable and perfect will of God, even the thing which is good and acceptable and perfect [in His sight for you]."* This applies wholeheartedly to us today; we don't have to conform to the world's view or opinion of us. We look to Christ to have Him define who we are as revealed in God's Word. We have the opportunity to have our minds renewed (change our self-talk) by repeating what He says about us as His children. He made us just the way He wanted us to be and He will enable us to discern His good, acceptable and perfect will. We can take on our new identity in Christ and we can become influencers of the world rather than being influenced by it.

Are you ready to be set free from comparing yourselves to others? Why?

_____

_____

_____

_____

_____

In addition to the damage of the lies and what the world expects us to be, we can take that one slippery step towards perfectionism.

I aimed for perfection because I was under the mistaken impression it was attainable. But thinking I had to be perfect made me fearful of making a mistake; I felt paralyzed. My understanding of perfectionism broadened when I read an article by Robin May, a licensed therapist and certified life coach. In her piece entitled, "The Truth about Perfectionism", she warns:

"The idea of 'perfectionism' can lead to serious challenges in life. Perfectionism demands that an individual be without any error, it places unrealistic expectations on one's performance and it leads to emotionally damaging self-criticism. It also puts too much weight on the perceptions of others. Lastly, and this is the one that really concerns me...it leads to the person striving for perfectionism to be judgmental of others who don't always get it right."[1]

This was quite an eye opener for me and it exactly described my challenges. Overwhelmed and overcome, I had to re-evaluate. With unrealistic expectations of what type of person I was supposed to be, all the voices that ran around in my head caused major damage and shattered many more pieces of my life. I cared way too much about what others would think of my shortcomings. Finally, ouch, the judgment I was placing on myself, I was also placing on others.

Do you struggle with perfectionism? If so, why?

_____

_____

_____

_____

_____

Studying God's Word helped me understand that only one person has ever lived a perfect life and that was Jesus. So how would I deal with my perfectionistic tendencies? The Apostle Paul serves as my example and inspiration. Even though he had made massive mistakes and he struggled with physical ailments, God used him to lead and shape the early Christian church and to author many books of the New Testament. Paul's letters inspired me and gave me hope, because I related in so many ways to his feelings. He states in *Philippians 3:11-13* (TLB), "*So whatever it takes, I will be one who lives in the fresh newness of life of those who are alive from the dead. I don't mean to say I am perfect. I haven't learned all I should even yet, but I keep working toward that day when I will finally be all that Christ saved me for and wants me to be. No, dear brothers, I am still not all I should be, but I am bringing all my energies to bear on this one thing: Forgetting the past and looking forward to what lies ahead*". I had to change my perspective away from perfectionism and become a woman who lived in the newness of life that God was restoring. I focused on His truth so that I could put the past behind me and look forward to the path that God has planned out ahead of me.

Are you willing to step into the fresh newness of life God has for you? Why?

_____

_____

_____

_____

_____

What will you do to replace those obnoxious, angry and mean tones with voices of grace, mercy and love?

_____

_____

_____

_____

_____

Through my intimate encounter with God at the women's retreat, my voice of fear was replaced with the voice of faith; I learned that standing alone was not a failure

Not only does the voice of faith begin to drown out the fear, but also the voices of doubt and rejection. God shows us that at times we have to be willing to take risks with our decisions and our hearts so that He can show how truly faithful His voice is.

As I shared earlier, Paul's words in *Romans 12:2* instruct us that we are not to conform to the ways of the world. We are transformed by the renewing of our minds in God's truth. By applying God's wisdom, we can begin to turn down the volume on those voices in our head, and we can begin to pick up the shattered broken pieces of our life that the accusing voices and lies have caused. Piece by piece, one by one God will find a way for us to be transformed and restored.

5 *Piece by Piece, One by One*

When all the shattered, broken pieces of your life are laying spread out all over the floor, it's hard to believe it is possible to pick up one of those sharp, jagged pieces, let alone all the other pieces. A poem, by William J. Egan, a recovering addict and poet speaks about picking up our lives piece by piece.

Piece by Piece[1]

My life is like one big puzzle right now...

I have to start putting it back together...

PIECE BY PIECE...

I will have to learn to love myself and eventually others will grow

to love me and slowly my life will come back together...

PIECE BY PIECE...

Gradually my life will become worth living...

My smile and my laugh will come back...

PIECE BY PIECE...

I will become someone people trust and they will take my word

for more than just a word because they will see I am putting my

life back together,

One moment at a time,

One Day At a time,

One piece at a time,

PIECE BY PIECE....

My opportunities will become my accomplishments,

My fear will become my past,

My outlook will always be optimistic,

My smile will never fade away,

My friends will become my family,

As long as I continue to take one step at time

One piece at a time,

My puzzle of life will come together...

PIECE BY PIECE

Like the words of the poem say, it's time to put our lives back together piece by piece. The advantage we have, as believers, is the promise that God will to help repair and restore each and every broken jagged piece. *Amos 9:11 (NLT) "In that day I will restore the fallen house of David. I will repair its damaged walls. From the ruins I will rebuild it and restore its former glory."*

In the process of rebuilding and restoring, we will likely revisit the pain again, but He will be there to comfort us, strengthen us and give us peace. In *John 14:27 (NLT)*, we can be comforted with the words of Jesus when He says, *"I am leaving you with a gift—peace of mind and heart. And the peace I give is a gift the world cannot give. So don't be troubled or afraid."*

Even with the promise of God's peace in the middle of my many jagged pieces, I still felt that I needed to protect myself from others. To keep others from seeing how broken and shattered I really was, I created an elaborate mask to distract them. My mask was happy, light-hearted, sweet, funny, and confident. It sparkled and shined so that others would be blinded from seeing the shattered, jagged pieces of my heart and soul beneath. I had worn the mask for so long that it had become glued to my face. Removing that protective mask would be almost impossible, because it would have meant that I would become fully exposed and beyond vulnerable.

Wouldn't it be wonderful if God would magically remove our masks and we could start over with a fresh, new, unbroken vision of ourselves? We may try to fool ourselves into believing that it is possible. But as I began to really study and absorb God's Word, He revealed to me that restoration was about removing and restoring not about replacing.

The Masquerade

Have you ever seen the movie "Mask--from Zero to Hero" with Jim Carrey? Jim Carrey's character is just an ordinary guy; but when he puts on an ancient mask, he becomes a magically powered trickster. He grows to think that this is the way he should be; but in the end he realizes that is not really who he wants to be. Isn't that the cunningness of the masks we put on ourselves-- we think that masks can disguise all of our hurt, pain, insecurities and shortcomings. We want to hide who we really are so we can be accepted and loved by the world's standards. From our multitude of masks, we can select the one that fits the situation and lets us fit with everyone else.

What are some of the masks you are putting on every day?

_____

_____

_____

_____

Oh, the mask I had created! It was beautiful and elaborate, shiny and sparkly. My mask had become a permanent fixture in my life, it was glued to my face. It was getting exhausting keeping that mask beautiful. I constantly tried to step over and ignore all my broken pieces, because each time I looked down and saw all the brokenness, my mask would dull. It finally became impossible not to look down as I slipped into that deep, dark pit. It was exhausting covering up my life-long imperfections, the enormous failure I truly believed I was, all my flawed and magnified insecurities, and the burden of my hurt and pain. All of these became the catalyst that broke down and stripped away the glue that kept my mask in place; and just like everything else in my life, my mask came crashing down and shattered on top of the jagged pieces of my life.

What does your mask(s) look like?

_____

_____

_____

_____

_____

Why do you think you can't take it off?

_____

_____

_____

_____

_____

_____

As my studying of God's Word continued, God guided me to Paul's second letter to the Corinthians. In *2 Corinthians 3:18 (TLB)*, he wrote *"But we Christians have no veil over our faces; we can be mirrors that brightly reflect the glory of the Lord. And as the Spirit of the Lord works within us, we become more and more like him."*

My Journal:

> *Oh Father I am so exhausted from trying to keep up all these masks I am juggling. I am so afraid to show who I really am. What if I am right that I am not worthy of people's love; and even worse, what if they don't think I am worthy either? What if they discover I am not perfect and they see how big a failure I really am? Is it time, Lord, for me to let my masks down? Will you be there to reassure me that keeping them down is what is right? Reveal to me, God, what is good about me, what is so special about me, and what you created me to be. Soften my heart and open my eyes to the beauty you see in me, because it is so hard for me to see.*

I was so relieved when God chose to show me (and He continues to show me) that dropping the masks and showing all of who I really am is not only acceptable, it is desirable. Revealing and facing my imperfections, my flaws, my failures, my insecurities, and my pain are the essential steps He is using to transform and restore me. My journey is a testimony of how He can transform pain to understanding and restore the broken to beautiful. Just as God graciously helped me to drop the masks and embark on this journey of restoration, He is waiting to do the same for you.   There is so much hope in embracing our true selves.

Let It Go

Have you ever watched a broken windshield being replaced? The process is methodical and fast. In order to remove the broken window, the technician goes around and around the edge of the windshield to loosen it. Once it is loose enough the damaged windshield is pulled out and replace with a smooth, sparkly one. That's how I wanted my life's transformation to be— painless and quick. However, God's redemptive plan involved tearing down and letting go of the remaining pieces of brokenness that were clinging to my life. This process proved to be as painful as the impact of the rocks that caused me to shatter in the first place.

I had to be strong to begin tearing down those painful pieces of my past that were so attached to my life. If I just kept circling around and around the edges of that the shattered pieces I thought that they could instantly repair themselves.

God directed me to be diligent and patient like the men who walked around the wall at Jericho waiting for the wall to fall. As the author of the book of _Hebrews 11:30_ writes, "_By faith the walls of Jericho fell, after the army had marched around them for seven days._" I had to have faith when the last pieces were being removed and dropped on the pile of already shattered pieces, I would be okay. Walking faithfully with Him, I grew confident that God would be there, that freedom would come as those last pieces fell. His love and mercy on my life would keep the restoration and healing process going. I was broken, with all my pieces exposed and jagged on the ground; I was ready to relinquish control and allow Him to take control of my life.

Letting go of those remaining pieces was an intense process; I was humbled and enlightened all at the same time. I had to acknowledge the pieces were still there clinging for dear life to that old frame; they needed to come down if I wanted to continue on the restorative journey.

**Are you willing to acknowledge you still have broken pieces still clinging on for dear life? What are they?**

_____

_____

_____

_____

Are you ready to let them go? Why?

_____

_____

_____

_____

_____

_____

My Journal:

> *God, why, why, why is it that I continue to be so stubborn? Why do I want to hold onto this pain and misery? I just can't believe I want to live this way. Open my eyes to something different; show me a way to get past this stupid stubbornness. I am sick and tired of this hurt. Please, please, please help!!!*

With all the pieces loose, it was time to take a look at each of those pieces lying on the ground--each of the lies.

Realize The Lies

Although it was penned thousands of years ago, *Psalms 55:11* aptly describes our modern world. *"Destructive forces are at work in the city; threats and lies never leave its streets."* Those destructive, diabolical forces, threats and lies are ever present. If this is our reality, how can we overcome them?

The lies do not go peacefully. Overcoming them takes daily attention; sometimes it is a minute-by-minute battle. Replacing lies with truth is an ongoing struggle for me. My first step to replacing all those lies was to acknowledge each one of them by writing pages and pages of them in my journal. I had so many lies to combat it was hard to know where to start. Earnest prayer and detailed journaling have become so important to me.

What are some of the lies you are telling yourself?

_____

_____

_____

_____

_____

_____

_____

My Journal:

> *God, I have lived with so many lies all my life, the lies of worthlessness, of not having value. The lies that fear whispers in my ear, "You are going to fail, you have been rejected your whole life, and everyone is so much better than you." I doubt my every good thought and good things that happens, thinking something bad has got to be right around the corner. The lies that I am not pretty enough,*

skinny enough, smart enough, or strong enough. All those lies, God, drove me into that deep, dark pit. How can I even see past the lies that leave me in this complete and utter darkness? Show me some light of your truth, God. Let that truth show me where to begin so that I can replace the lies. I am leaving it in your hands to show me where the light of your truth starts.

Another entry:

Wow, God, I have become overwhelmed by what studying your word daily is teaching and showing me. Will those truths help me take steps out of the darkness? Your words are becoming the cracks of light I needed to start guiding me out of the darkness. Keep me studying, Lord, keep revealing every bit of truth your word has for me as I am climbing out of the pit I have been keeping myself in... I pray, Lord, that you continue to replace the darkness of the lies with the light of your truth.

God has led me into the light of His truth daily to learn to combat the lies that want to keep me in darkness. He specifically shows me daily the lies I need to overcome through the wisdom and knowledge found in His Word. The unfolding of the restoration process keeps replacing the darkness of lies with the light of His truth. This book you are now reading is a result of the process. We continually struggle with feelings of worthlessness, negative self-image, and insignificance, but how do we allow Him to reveal His love our true, worthy, valuable and significant image in His sight. The voices of fear, doubt, rejection, comparison and perfection-ism are quieted with truth. We are fearless with Him; confident and wanted, unique and special. He guides the process of picking up the pieces and He selects the next piece to be put back in its proper place. It is a constant battle to combat new lies the enemy sends to assault our minds. Let us keep before our eyes the real vision of the woman He created.

Are you ready to replace the lies with truth? Why?

_____

_____

_____

_____

_____

The next step was twofold--prayer and journaling. As He began to reveal His truth and answers my prayers, it became even more important to journal them. Acknowledging, comparing and replacing the lies with truth has been a crucial component of picking up each of those broken and shattered pieces. The journey begins the moment you pick up the first piece and you realize you are not alone in this courageous restoring process--He is there.

As I accepted God's truth, I began to see that I was not still allowing all of God's truth to fully penetrate my heart. The next step in the restoration process was to learn His truth about forgiving the unforgivable

6 Forgiving the Unforgivable

A week after my mom passed away, I was doing housework with my grandmother, when she blindsided me with these devastating words. "You realize you are the one who caused your mother's death, don't you?" The sharpness of her blaming words was a huge boulder the size of a house; it broke me. Paralyzed by the shock, I couldn't move. Instantly, my inner voice accused me. "You are a terrible person. Your mom couldn't even love you, so what makes you think your grandmother would? You are worthless. You caused your mother such misery that it led to her death." In my shock, I realized that both my mom and grandmother were so impossibly unloving that they seemed unforgivable. But God knew that forgiveness was a vital key to my journey to be healed and restored.

Forgiveness is a big, scary word. We resist the concept because neither giving nor receiving forgiveness is anywhere near comfortable. But God was not interested in my comfort. He wanted to transform me, and forgiveness was essential. My hardened heart prevented me from forgiving others, and my deep hurt and anger made me feel unworthy to receive the forgiveness from Him or to forgive myself.

Withholding forgiveness made me feel powerful. I would give forgiveness only when I felt that whomever had hurt me had been punished to my satisfaction. Such an unhealthy place to be! When I was holding on to all that anger, hurt, frustration, doubt, fear, pain and sadness, neither happiness nor satisfying relationships were possible.

When significant hurt starts when you are a child and the rocks continue to be thrown at you into adulthood, the constant pain can lead to unforgiveness. When we hold forgiveness hostage, it can take us spiraling down to a deeply depressing place. This was where I found myself. Of all the areas I had to work on, being able to forgive was among the biggest. I had to stare it down, accept it and give it if I were going to move forward toward transformation.

For me, complete forgiveness had three parts: asking God's forgiveness, offering myself forgiveness, and forgiving those who had hurt me. I had to seek God's forgiveness for all that I had done and all that I had held back from Him. Forgiving myself meant letting go of all the persecution, fault, and blame I placed on myself for my mistakes and failures. Finally, I had to forgive others who had hurt me and contributed to my brokenness.

Asking for and receiving God's forgiveness, was the place I chose to start.

Forgiven

For years I was aware that God sent His only Son to save me from sin and I knew that He forgave me. My mind knew, but my heart had not experienced that forgiveness.

My Journal:

> *Why in the world would God want to have this broken, unworthy and complete failure of a woman in a personal relationship with Him? Why would He even want to give me the time of day? Do I deserve you, God? Do I deserve your forgiveness?*

It was a struggle for me to accept God's forgiveness. Could I really and truly believe that He had forgiven me? As I made my slow climb out of the dark pit, *Acts 13:38* spoke loudly to my heart. *"Therefore, my friends, I want you to know that through Jesus the forgiveness of sins is proclaimed to you."* It was proclaimed to me, and when I finally decided to accept His forgiveness, it became my new reality. I am forgiven for all that I have ever done that displeased Him, and I can ask for His forgiveness when I fall short in the future.

The truth of *John 3:16* penetrated deep into my being. It reads, *"For God so loved the world that He gave His one and only Son, that whoever believes in Him shall not perish but have eternal life."* On that cross, Jesus bore the penalty for each and every one of the sins we have ever committed and for those sins we will commit in the future. *Matthew 26:28* reassures us of God's forgiveness: *"This is my blood of the covenant, which is poured out for many for the forgiveness of sins."* God desires that we believe that this truth applies to us, even when we feel we are not deserving of that forgiveness.

We receive even more encouragement from *Acts 26:18*, in which God instructs the Apostle Paul to preach the good news that God wants *"to open their eyes and turn them from darkness to light, and from the power of Satan to God, so that they may receive forgiveness of sins and a place among those who are sanctified by faith in me."* Could I apply this to me? Could it be true for you? If God can take me from complete darkness and show me the brilliant hope of His light, what empowerment could you possibly receive? I have the power through Him to experience "sanctification,"; that's a big word that refers to the Holy Spirit's influence in preparing believers for eternity. He gives us the power to turn away from the complete despair and darkness, and walk toward the light of His hope--His forgiveness.

My Journal:

> *Dear God, please forgive me! I have been so unhappy that I have caused myself to pull away from everyone who loved me and truly wants what is best for me, including you! I have hardened my heart. It has always been easier to push everyone, including you, away so that you didn't have to see my pain and hurt. I have pretended for so long to be that perfect girl who had it all together. No one could break through my hard heart. I am sorry for hurting those around me because of my own hurt. Forgive me, Lord, for not being the woman you had planned for me to be.*

Luke 1:77 tells us that he desires *"to give His people the knowledge of salvation through the forgiveness of their sins."* It's time to release our burdens, ask for forgiveness, and allow ourselves to experience this beautiful gift from God.

Are there some things in your life that you have been holding on to because you don't think you deserved God's forgiveness? What are they?

_____

_____

_____

_____

_____

Deserving of Forgiveness

Being open to forgive ourselves can be an enormous challenge. I blamed and shamed myself for decades for not living up to the standards and expectations that others had of me. I added my own condemning voice. Since I thought I didn't deserve God's forgiveness, why would I ever think about forgiving myself?

Jesus bore the weight of the world's sin on Himself. I was overwhelmed by His proclamation at the end *John 19:30* which says, *"... Jesus said, 'It is finished.' With that, He bowed His head and gave up His spirit."* If He said forgiveness was accomplished, then I had an obligation to give forgiveness as well.

I was going to have to forgive myself. Grace, mercy and love were God's gifts to me; I needed to grant myself permission to receive them. He had forgiven all my selfish actions, impure thoughts, and judgmental behaviors. If God could forgive me of all the things I had done and not keep track of them, I needed to give myself that gift.

In what areas do you need to forgive yourself?

_____

_____

_____

_____

_____

It has been hard to let go of my self-condemnation; I ask Him daily to open my eyes and my heart to the areas where I need to acknowledge His forgiveness. I need to let to go and let God wipe away my guilt. I am worth so much more than blaming and shaming myself for the past.

My Journal:

> *...Lord, allow me to forgive myself for being so hard on myself for all my failures and mistakes; for all the condemning thoughts that I have trained myself to believe. Would you give me the eyes to see me how you see me? I am sure I will not believe you at first; but please continue to show me that I can see myself in a new way. Show me how I can give myself the grace that you give me.*

Forgiving the Unforgivable

I withheld forgiveness from two women in my life--my mom and my maternal grandmother. My mother's own pain kept her so emotionally unavailable that I went through my childhood and my teenage years feeling unloved and unwanted. I felt like I was an inconvenience for her; I could never live up to her expectations. Her emotional pain increased during my sophomore year of high school when she was diagnosed with breast cancer and underwent surgery and treatment. Her remission was short lived and she developed brain cancer. In the summer before my senior year of high school, the cancer took her life. I was so angry with her--the way she had made me feel all those years, but now that she was gone, I felt even angrier that she had abandoned me.

It was during that same painful summer that my grandmother blamed me for my mother's death. My response was not to do drugs, drink, or party. I turned my fury inward and let her words reinforce all the negative things I had felt and believed. I couldn't fathom forgiving either of them, which created the cracks of my pain to grow deeper. When God confronted me with this unforgiveness, I asked, "Why would I want to forgive them?" I had spent years trying to build a relationship with each of them because that's what I thought I was supposed to do; after all they were my mom and grandma.

Hurt and bitterness overtook me and I closed my heart and mind to them. There was no way I would ever consider forgiving either my mother or my grandmother.

A couple of years ago, I met a wise woman who completely changed my thinking about forgiveness. She had experienced horrific and unimaginable things; yet even she was finally able to forgive those who had caused her extraordinary pain. Here is her incredibly valuable lesson:

> "Forgiveness is not for the person who caused the pain, forgiveness is for you. You are not punishing them, because they likely don't even acknowledge their wrong-doing. They go on living their lives and we live with bitterness and hurt in our hearts, which only hurts us."[1]

What an "AHA" moment for me! After this revelation, it would still take some time for me to finally let go and forgive. The bitterness of unforgiveness was lifted when I finally decided to write a letter to my mom letting her know that I had forgiven her. I let her know that I understood why she treated me the way she did. *My letter to my mom:*

Dear Mom,

I love you and I miss having a mom in my life. I am sorry that you didn't get to see me get married, meet your grandchildren, and especially for missing the chance for us to mend our relationship.

Mom, you hurt me so deeply! You made me feel so unwanted, that I didn't deserve to be loved and that there was nothing I could ever do to make you love me. I wanted so badly to earn your love, but I constantly fell short. Why couldn't you just love me? I now know not why, it is because you never wanted me in the first place. It all made sense when the revelation of you wishing you could have aborted me came to light. I was so mad, bitter and angry at you for making me feel this way and I wanted to hold on to all the hurt, anger, resentment, shame and guilt.

Mom, I want to thank you for not aborting me. Although you couldn't give me the love that I so desperately wanted, I can look back now and be thankful. I know all the hurt and pain I experienced can be used in a way that will allow me to inspire other women. I spent so long feeling unworthy, unloved and unwanted; but now I know how worthy, loved and wanted I am by God. He has filled the hole in my heart with His love.

Mom, I forgive you!

Although my grandmother is still alive, I did not want to see her in person to grant my forgiveness, because I thought that I needed to re-establish a relationship with her. But I learned a second lesson from the wise woman that taught me about toxic relationships and forgiveness. In a toxic relationship, one person repeatedly verbally or physically assaults the other person leading to a severe hurt and damage. Re-establishing a toxic relationship is not necessary for forgiveness to take place. Knowing this, I gave myself permission to forgive my grandmother. Blessings came when I forgave their words and actions toward me. Feelings of bitterness, anger and unforgiveness did not control my life anymore. Don't get me wrong, sometimes the thoughts still flood my brain; but I can more rapidly see them as lies and dismiss them.

As I walk more closely with God, I discover more about the freedom that forgiveness offers. And He continues to reveal to me more people to whom I need to extend forgiveness. God's forgiveness is unconditional and I need to follow His lead in forgiving others and myself.

Who do you need to forgive in your life?

_____

_____

_____

_____

I hope forgiveness is a less scary word now. When you pursue forgiveness in all its aspects, you will find that true freedom is waiting for you.

God offers us this beautiful gift of His Son, who was sacrificed so that we could experience the greatness of His love for us. We can be forgiven and receive His mercy, grace, and unconditional love. Accept this precious gift of forgiveness He offers to you and give that gift to others.

Once we accept that God can forgive us, it is time for us to turn His grace, mercy and love on ourselves. We need to forgive ourselves and let go. Allow Him to replace shame, guilt and failure with the powerful truth of what He has destined for us.

Finally, to receive our full forgiveness, we must forgive others. God forgave all of our mistakes, failures and pain, what right do we have to withhold forgiveness from others?

I pray that you experience this amazing gift of forgiveness for yourself. Once you have learned to give and receive forgiveness, true transformation is possible.

7 Transformation is Possible

Have you ever listened to a song and it's telling your story? How could anyone else ever know the depth of your pain? The lyrics to Big Daddy Weave's song, "Redeemed", sums up my story beautifully.

Redeemed[1]

Seems like all I can see was the struggle

Haunted by ghosts that lived in my past

Bound up in shackles of all my failures

Wondering how long is this gonna last

Then You look at this prisoner and say to me "son

stop fighting a fight that's already been won"

I am redeemed, You set me free

So I'll shake off theses heavy chains

Wipe away every stain now I'm not who I used to be

I am redeemed

All my life I have been called unworthy
Named by the voice of my shame and regret
But when I hear You whisper, "Child lift up your head"
I remember oh God, You're not done with me yet

I don't have to be the old man inside of me
Cause his day is long dead and gone
I've got a new name, a new life I'm not the same
And a hope that will carry me home

To believe that transformation is possible, we have to realize that the fight has already been won by the unconditional love of Jesus's death covering our sins. The heavy chains that hold us back are the feelings of fear and worthlessness coupled with the reluctance to forgive the pains of our past. Stepping out of our shame, regret, failures and struggles, we can allow God to lift up our heads to see the beautiful gift of hope He has given. As our transformation progresses, we are constantly growing and changing. The Apostle Paul shares with us in his first letter to the Corinthians, saying in *1 Corinthians 15:37-40* (CEV) "*Wheat seeds and all other seeds look different from the sprouts that come up. This is because God gives everything the kind of body he wants it to have. People, animals, birds, and fish are each made of flesh, but none of them are alike. Everything in the heavens has a body, and so does everything on earth. But each one is very different from all the others."* These verses are the realization that we can be transformed. We start out one way, for me it was, broken and shattered. Then when we truly accept Him into our hearts, He can transform us to the bodies, heart, mind and soul He designed. Created special and unique, unlike any other. Our wonderful, complete transformation will occur when we meet Jesus face to face.

We are new creations, beautiful daughters, when we open our hearts to the power of His redemption. There is still work to be done in order for us to realize and really accept our identities and enjoy the fullness and richness that comes with them. In *2 Corinthians 5:17 (TLB)* it says, *"When someone becomes a Christian, he becomes a brand new person inside. He is not the same anymore. A new life has begun!"* How amazing it is that we can become brand new and leave behind the broken person we used to be.

When we give ourselves permission to move forward on this new path, we step out of the quicksand that threatened to swallow us. We can trust our loving God to faithfully guide us.

Our renewal involves restoring trust in ourselves, in others, and even in God. As trust is being reestablished in our lives, we are free to move towards the goal of becoming the women God envisioned.

Trust One More Time

When we have been deeply hurt by someone whom we have trusted, it is really hard to recover from that. Those jagged pieces are so difficult to restore. My mom broke my trust because her words and actions caused profound hurt and sadness at the core of my heart. The sharp edge of that broken trust caused me to second-guess everything and everyone.

Can you name people in your life who have broken your trust? Make a list.

_____

_____

_____

_____

_____

Are you willing to begin restoring trust with them? Why?

_____

_____

_____

_____

_____

_____

How can trust be restored with someone, like my mother, who has passed on? Well, for me it was the same process as forgiveness. With God's help, I had to let go of the control that mistrust had on me. I had to allow the hurt and pain to be wiped away. What do you do if the person or persons are still in your life? Perhaps you are allowing bitterness and anger to build. You are thinking that they should make the first move, since they are the ones who caused the hurt. Let's be honest: if you wait for them to come to you, you could be waiting forever. The helpful advice I received from my friend about forgiveness also applies to restoring trust-- it is not necessary to re-enter a toxic relationship to shed the mistrust. By initiating the restoration process, we become like the people whom the Old Testament prophet Isaiah spoke about in *Isaiah 58:12* *"Your people will rebuild the ancient ruins and will raise up the age-old foundations; you will be called Repairer of Broken Walls, Restorer of Streets with Dwellings."* It is up to us to rebuild and repair our ruins; we will be called to be the repairers of broken trust and restorers of the shattered pieces.

If you have struggled with your trust in God, I understand. There were times when my trust in God wavered, because He had allowed people to wound and break me.

My Journal:

> *God, I sometimes don't understand the hurt and the pain; how could you allow me to bear this weight that suffocates me. I placed my trust in you and I feel like you have abandoned me. What I have done wrong, Lord? Why am I falling back into my old patterns? Why do I let the enemy in so easily that I can change on a dime the relationship we have built? Lord, restore my hope and trust in you, even though I know I don't deserve it.*

I spent my entire life trying to be in control and not letting anyone help me. I didn't know who I could trust, including God. As I shared in my journal, when I faced pain, I wondered how He could allow it. Early in my walk with God, I tested him constantly; I wanted to see if I could trust Him, even in the pain. If you are struggling to trust not only yourself, but others and God, be assured that He will not give up on you. He is the Restorer and He can repair and restore your broken shattered pieces of trust back where they belong. If you begin to doubt His trustworthiness, consider the sound wisdom from *Proverbs 3:5-6* *"Trust in the LORD with all your heart and lean not on your own understanding; in all your ways submit to him, and He will make your paths straight."* Trust Him with the process and allow restored trust to enrich your life. Even when you are rebuilding trust, you must believe that trust and transformation are possible.

Permission Granted

Are you struggling with giving yourself permission to move forward? Are you letting your hurt, bitterness, and anger (even maybe a few more) stop you in your tracks? I surely did. I struggled with giving myself the permission to move forward, because I was letting all my emotions control me. This quote by Iyanla Vanzant, author and inspiration speaker, gave me that little spark I needed.

> "I gave myself permission to feel and experience all of my emotions. In order to do that, I had to stop being afraid to feel. In order to do that, I taught myself to believe that no matter what I felt or what happened when I felt it, I would be okay."[2]

A crucial step in our growth is giving ourselves permission to experience our emotions--good and bad. We need to find a way to fearlessly express these strong feelings and emotions. One of the primary reasons I journal is so that I can pour out my heart on paper. God's Word teaches that He is our Father and He wants us to share with Him our deepest concerns. As it says in *1 Peter 5:7, "Cast all your anxiety on Him because he cares for you."* No matter what we are feeling or experiencing, He is not going to reject us, He cares way too much.

Opening our hearts and taking risks are both important ways we give ourselves permission to move towards trans-formation. We must risk opening our hearts to God and others or we will not experience all the fullness and richness that God has planned for us. Yes, by opening our hearts, we risk being hurt again; but now we have tools to handle the hurt. Taking risks to trust can usher in the biggest blessings and rewards God wants give to us.

My Journal:

> *I am taking a big leap of faith today, Lord. I am going WAY OUT of my comfort zone! I am beginning to see the vision you are creating in me and it scares me to death. I have to take the risk to get in the race, Lord, even when I know the past wants to prevent me from doing it. I am scared to be hurt again. Show me the reward that this risk can bring to me. Lord, let it be so great that I cannot help but risk it all for you!*

Are you willing to take the risk to live a life that God has intended for you? What is that risk?

_____

_____

_____

Having given yourself permission to move forward, now is the time to become the "real you" God designed you to be.

Will the Real You Please Stand Up

"The thing that is really hard, and really amazing, is giving up on being perfect and beginning the work of becoming yourself."[3] Anna Quindlen, author, journalist.

Can you say "OUCH!" I shared earlier about my struggles with perfectionism. However, I have to remind myself regularly that I am on a journey to maturity; I have to give up on trying to be sinless. Sinless perfection has not been nor will it ever be my human earthly reality.

Becoming the real you requires that you pick up the pieces that lay scattered all over the floor and take off your bright, shiny, perfect masks. It is about individually addressing the experience and hurt that each piece represents. With healing, each piece can be restored and your life will be better than you believed possible.

Becoming the authentic you means surrendering your damaged self to God, asking for His help, and rejoicing as He reveals what the restored and transformed you will look like.

Becoming the radiant, restored real you requires that you give and receive forgiveness. Don't hold on to bitterness and anger; they will hold you back from hope and freedom that forgiveness offers.

What is holding you back from becoming the "real you"?

_____

_____

_____

_____

_____

It's time to let the "real you" stand up and be noticed! Be courageous enough to pursue the desires of your heart-- praying big, believing in God-sized dreams, and walking toward the purpose God planned for you before you were even born.

8 Our Heart Must Go On

Waking up one morning, you have a feeling that something is going to be different. Months of struggle, patience and perseverance have left you running on empty. You're not sure that you will be able to endure another day of the emotional jumping jacks that you have been doing over and over. The next morning, there is a peace that you can't quite explain; you wonder if this is the calm before another storm. Then, the next morning you experience that same peace, but on top of that you feel an elevated sense of hope. How long will this upward trend continue? The next morning you have the same peace, the new level of hope, and now you get a glimpse of a new future. For the first time in forever, you can focus on your dreams and stop worrying about the struggle. God has planted seeds of desires in your heart and faith will make them grow.

This was my experience not long ago. Before this time, I had stopped believing in the possibility of dreams. I was so unlike my husband who is a dreamer, goal setter, and a big-vision kind of person. While I have always admired him, I could not imagine myself as ever having those qualities. But on that amazing morning, my eyes and heart were opened to the possibility that the dreams and desires God was giving me would come true.

God's gifts, plans, and purposes for us take shape as the desires of our heart. Reaching this point reaffirms to me that all the really hard struggles, pain, and hurt from our past are starting to heal, our hearts may go on to pursue these desires.

It is time to step into the race that God has given to us to run and win. As global evangelist, Christine Caine says, in her bestseller, *Unstoppable*, "God calls you to step into the race not because you are mighty and strong. He calls you to take your place in the race because He is mighty and strong and He plans to accomplish His work in and through You." [1]

My Journal:

Lord, thank you for giving me the desire and the ability to read again. The book I am currently reading is exactly what I need to be hearing right now. You knew that I needed sports metaphors to show me how to step towards the life you are creating for me. I have to get up to the starting line of the path and purpose you are creating for me. I have to get myself in the race. I have to stop sitting on the sidelines, because I am afraid to make mistakes. I am afraid to get in the race and risk failing. I know about winning and losing; and for the first time in a really long time, Lord, I am ready for finally experience winning. I have been losing for so long. Thank you, God, for the planting the seed in my heart to feel hopeful again.

What seeds do you think God is planting in you?

_____

_____

_____

_____

_____

Are you starting to see the hope of the desires of your heart? What are they?

_____

_____

_____

_____

_____

"Take delight in the LORD, and He will give you the desires of your heart." Psalms 37:4. As we start the race to pursue the

desires of our hearts, we develop new patterns of thought and behavior. Moving into God's plans and purpose for our lives, our vision expands and so does the need for bigger prayers.

Our bigger prayers become the water that nourishes those seeds of desire, the dreams that God uses to open our heart to a big picture vision of what He has in store for us. His dreams for us can and will come true.

As those fed and watered seeds grow, we begin to reap the harvest that blesses not only us, but for others around us. God's plan and purpose provides the fruit for us to share.

Are you willing to water and grow the seeds of dreams and desires God has given you? Why?

_____

_____

_____

_____

_____

What dreams is God giving you, that you might have ignored before?

_____

_____

_____

_____

Pray Beyond Possible

In Mark Batterson's book, *The Circle Maker*, he makes a bold statement, "The greatest tragedy in life is the prayers that go unanswered because they go unasked."[2] I admit that my prayer life started off with simple, self-centered, infrequent prayers. I would ask for help, seek answers, thank Him for revelation, and move on.

But on the morning when hope began, I knew I was going to have to step up my prayer life. I had experienced firsthand the tragedy of unasked prayer, by allowing my fear of failure and negative self-talk to prevent and diminish the desires and dreams that God was giving me. I was missing the many opportunities and gifts because I could not see through all the broken and shattered pieces of my heart. I could not possibly be worthy or valuable enough to receive anything, so I did not even ask. I am learning to ask those prayers as I become braver and bolder in my relationship with God.

What desires or dreams could you not be seeing because of your brokenness?

_____

_____

_____

_____

What prayers didn't you ask because you were afraid?

_____

_____

_____

_____

_____

My Journal:

> _Dear God, can I really ask for bigger things? Do you really think I am ready to handle them? I am worthy to even ask for something bigger; you have provided me with so much already. I am feeling this stirring in my heart, I wanting things that I never thought could be possible. Is it really you or am I just wanting it so badly that I am thinking it is you. Give me the eyes to see and the heart to feel what it is you are giving me to pray bigger about. Let me see your vision and not my own._

What if God answers my big prayers? What could that possibly mean for me and others? Continuing in Mark Batterson's book, _The Circle Maker_, he gives the following insight:

> "Prayer doesn't just change circumstances; more importantly it changes us. It doesn't just alter external realities; it alters internal realities so that we see with spiritual eyes. It gives us peripheral vision. It corrects our

nearsightedness. It enables us to see beyond our circumstances, beyond ourselves, beyond time."[3]

By taking this insight to heart, I was able to see past what was right in front of me, lift my head up, and see beyond all my brokenness. I put my selfishness aside and I let God lead. I saw that the plan and purpose were bigger than I could have possibly imagined--a bigger vision beyond the here and right now. He allowed me to see the changes He had made in me; this gave me the ability to see my past circumstances differently. Changing the way I saw things by looking at them through the eyes of God, I saw healing and restoration.

The restoration process is hard work. You have seen bits and pieces of the work I have already done, but in all honesty I am still at work on it today. Among the many changes I have implemented in my life, one stands above the rest. Mark Batterson puts it this way, "I work like it depends on me, but pray like it depends on God."[4]

My Journal:

The work continues today, Lord. Sometimes I just want to give up and stop working so hard! But I know that I have to keep working, keep pressing on. You have that great big plan and dream for me, Lord, and I want to see it become a reality. So I am going to keep working and praying even harder so that your vision can become my reality.

When you are working on dreams that God has given you, it is wise to create an action plan, set goals, and take steps to put the plan into action while always remembering to pray every step of the way. Without diligent prayer, we will wander off the path. A wrong step in the plan, a misguided goal, or thinking "I've got this" can head us in the wrong direction. When unexpected turns blindside us, we can pause and thank God for stopping us from following a selfish plan.

God guides us back on His path by refocusing our attention and changing our course. At times I got really frustrated! God has had to refocus me many times. I am learning to be more diligent in praying over the plan, so I can be in alignment with God's purpose.

It is so important for us not to give up too easily, too soon, or to stop praying before God has a chance to do His work. In the *Mark 11:24*, we read these words, *"Therefore I tell you, whatever you ask for in prayer, believe that you have received it, and it will be yours."* There are some prayers He has not yet answered; I am still waiting to see if or when He might make them a reality. Of course, I get frustrated and impatient when I am praying big prayers and nothing seems to be happening. But I keep growing and learning as I continue to work like it depends on me and keep praying like it depends on Him.

What prayers do you see beyond possible?

_____

_____

_____

_____

_____

What plan do you have to put each one of these into action?

_____

_____

_____

_____

God-Sized Dreams

"Prayer and imagination are directly proportional; the more you pray, the bigger your imagination becomes because the Holy Spirit supersizes it with God-sized dreams. Dreaming is a form of praying, and praying is a form of dreaming. The more you pray the bigger your dreams will become. And the bigger your dreams become the more you will have to pray."[5] Mark Batterson.

Do these statements make you a little nervous? Okay, a lot

nervous, like they did me? My nervousness came from fear, doubt and wondering if I was worthy of the responsibility of having God-sized dreams. I had to stop myself and realize that I was not going to have to make these dreams a reality by myself; the Holy Spirit was going to help me. I have heard it said that God doesn't call the equipped, He equips the called. God would equip me for whatever dreams He was calling me to.

My Journal:

> *Do you really feel I am ready, God, to have such big dreams? You are giving me numbers that I can't even begin to fathom the impact that could have. Do you really think my story is worth sharing? Is the dream, that it could impact and change the lives of women, really something I could do? That is way beyond what I was thinking God. That takes this to a whole new level. You are equipping me right????? The story is yours to tell and I am just the vessel for the story. Ok, I am going to go out on a limb here, Lord. Dear Father, I come to you today in prayer that you will give me the strength for the incredible vision you have shown me. The story you have written through my pain will have great impact and bring hope and transformation for all your beautiful, wonderful daughters.*

Another entry:

> *Ok, God, what are you thinking? Why am I getting this feeling that I am going to write a book? This is not one of my talents. Lord, you know the only reason I made it through high school English was because of Cliff Notes. You want me to do what???!! Well, God, I guess if this is the way I need to share my story, then you are going to have to be the one to write it! You know my strengths and weaknesses; and this is not one of my strengths. There is comfort in knowing that I can tell the story. I will rely on you and the Holy Spirit to do the rest! Ok, God, let's do this!*

I started to feel like a little kid who has a bright, vivid, colorful imagination. God-sized dreams drew me to pray and pray big. The idea that dreaming is a form of praying baffled me at first. Then as I thought about it more, I became more inspired. Now, let's not escape to far from reality, those fears and doubts can still try to sneak in and rob me of those God-sized dreams or any dreams for that matter. A few times I cried because I feared that these big dreams would overwhelm me and I wouldn't be up to the task to bring them to reality. It was in those times that I needed to ground myself in His Word. I was reminded of how much grace, mercy, forgiveness, and unconditional love He has.

What God-sized dreams do you have?

_____

_____

_____

_____

_____

What big prayers are you going to pray to see those God-sized dreams become reality?

_____

_____

_____

_____

_____

It is time for us to let child-like wonder, dreams, and imagination back into our lives! It is time to start praying and dreaming big and bold!

Our Mess is Our Message

"I cry out to God Most High, to God who will fulfill his purpose for me." _Psalms 57:2 (NLT)_. I have lived and experienced this verse. I shared earlier that I challenged God to show me my purpose. Before my fall into the deep darkness, He had shown me that "Dress with Purpose" was part of His purpose for me. When I started to get comfortable and think I could do it on my own, He pointed me to *Proverbs 19:21 (NLT)* which states, *"You can make many plans, but the LORD's purpose will prevail."* I didn't know it, but the truth of this verse was about to play out in my life in a dramatic way.

As I stared at the pill bottle, it seemed like taking the pills would be a quick solution to my endless pain. My mind was tortured by the lies that everything that I had ever done was worthless, that I wasn't deserving of feeling loved, and that my life had no value. That deep, dark place that I thought would swallow me alive was all part of God's plan to get my attention. When we face those really hard times, when things seem hopeless, when we lose faith that God is there, it is part of the purpose. We may ask why and I did.

The darkness I experienced and the climb I have endured out of that place made God's purpose for me abundantly clear.

My Journal:

> *Ok God, I get it!!! I am ready to work this journey to share my story; I am ready to lay it all out there, Lord. Raw and exposed. These past few months have taught me that I need to rely on You and not on me. The clarity of the vision is refreshing and inspiring. I understand that I am to help women walk through their brokenness, to discover the beautiful identity you have for them; I know this is it,*

because this is exactly what you have done for me. You have placed the seed in my heart to share this amazing gift with others so they too can see that there is hope to escape that deep, dark, cold pit that they have allowed themselves to slip into. You shone your light on me when I cried out to you. You can help me inspire and encourage women that the same light is available for them.

"And we know that God causes everything to work together for the good of those who love God and are called according to his purpose for them." Romans 8:28 (NLT) Even when it doesn't seem like His plan and purpose will become clear to us, we have hope in the fact that He does work everything together for good. It took me 45 years to figure out my true purpose, so there is always hope!

"The thief's purpose is to steal and kill and destroy. My purpose is to give them a rich and satisfying life." John 10:10 (NLT). We must not allow the thief to steal, kill or destroy the rich and satisfying life God has called us to live.

Transformational life change comes by learning to pray big, see God-sized dreams, and live in the purpose He created for us. As we move towards transformation, we will start to see the vivid, colorful, beautiful identity the He has waiting for us to claim.

There is no limit to what God can do through us; what we might think is impossible, God makes possible. We can become the God kind of beautiful women He created.

9 Be God's Kind of Beautiful

On the way to discovering our beautiful identity in God, we have to take a journey of walking tirelessly and blindly through the valleys of hurt and pain, trudging the paths of forgiveness and healing, persevering step by step up the mountain until we reach the summit of restoration and ultimately transformation.

We have walked out quite a long and amazing journey so far. My journey began four years ago and the beautiful identity God created for me is still unfolding. His plan and purpose are complex and simple, hard and easy, sad and happy, angry and peaceful, dark and light, but most of all insightful and rewarding. The journey out of darkness into God's light is one of the greatest gifts I have received. As we start to respond to our gifts and talents, we will experience increased joy and fulfillment.

When we become attuned to God's purpose for us, He will

reveal our spiritual gifts and the fruit of His Spirit will become more evident in our thoughts and actions. Discovering the talents we were born with is exciting and scary, because He intends for us to start putting them into practice to accomplish His purposes. Slowly, we begin to see a shift from self-confidence, to God-Confidence.

As we seek and find the light of God's purpose, He will continue to refine us.

Diamond in the Rough

Do you know how a diamond is created? It starts out as an oddly shaped, black lump of coal underground. The earth applies extreme pressure and stress until a rough diamond is formed. The rough diamond is mined, but its beauty is still unseen. A master diamond cutter skillfully removes the dark exterior to reveal the brilliant stone. A rough diamond can be cut into many beautiful, sparkly, polished diamonds. Diamonds, by nature, have flaws and imperfections. Some have many and others have fewer, yet they are still beautiful. Picture your life as one of God's diamonds in the rough. Just as a rough diamond does not refine itself, neither do we refine ourselves—that's God's job, He is the master diamond cutter.

I started this journey as the black, lump of coal. The pressure, stress, and circumstances of life weighed heavily on me.

I did not know that God was able to use hurtful and painful experiences to create a diamond in the rough. When the time was right, God took me out of the depths of my old broken life and brought me to His master cutting area to begin chipping away the darkness, hurt, and pain. As He was working diligently in my life, I was being refined into beautiful, sparkly, and polished diamond, with all my flaws and imperfections. I have experienced an incredible transformation at the hand of the master craftsman-- God.

A lot of hard work has been done so far, and we might think we have arrived and the hard work is over. I don't want to disillusion you or burst you bubble, but there is still more work to be done.

We may still stumble and fall back into our old patterns and beliefs about ourselves. In those times, we start to lose our polish, beauty and sparkle. Yet God is there to pick us up and re-polish and make us sparkle for His glory again. Our gifts and talents can once again shine brilliantly. He allows us to transition from ordinary to extraordinary.

You Are Not Ordinary

Leo Buscaglia, PhD, an author and speaker, is quoted as saying, "Your talent is God's gift to you. What you do with it is your gift back to God."[1] Perhaps you were like me, I had no idea what gifts and talents God had given me.

My Journal:

> *God, I am confused! I hear you and I know that you are calling me to share my story, but I don't know how. I know you must have some idea how this is going to get done. I don't think I have what it takes, God, especially since you want me to share this message with lots of women. I know that you will equip me, but I have to have some sort of talent for you to build on, right????*

Shortly after this journal entry I attended my normal early morning Sunday church service at my where my pastor, Dr. Jim Garlow, was teaching about identifying our gifts and talents. That afternoon I turned to Google and found a Spiritual Gifts Assessment at www.spiritualgiftstest.com. The results report an individual's strongest gifting and how the person ranks in the other gifts as well. I encourage you to take the test and share your results and thoughts in your journal.

My Journal:

> *God, you are so funny! Pastor Jim spoke in church today about gifts and talents. I guess I need to go find out more about the talents and gifts you created in me. He gave us a couple of resources and I am going to check it out. Am I*

going to be surprised, God? Will they be anything to build my confidence? You must have something there for me God… I took the test this afternoon and I was surprised and shocked by the results. Leadership. Administration. Faith. Teaching. Are you SURE???? What I am going to do with these God???

As you can see, at first I wasn't sure the results of the test were right. If I took it again, would results be the same? Once I was comfortable that the test results were correct, I set out to explore and fully understand my talents and gifts so that I could use them to fulfill my calling. In *1 Corinthians 12:4-11*, the Apostle Paul instructs us:

"There are different kinds of gifts, but the same Spirit distributes them. There are different kinds of service, but the same Lord. There are different kinds of working, but in all of them and in everyone it is the same God at work. Now to each one the manifestation of the Spirit is given for the common good. To one there is given through the Spirit a message of wisdom, to another a message of knowledge by means of the same Spirit, to another faith by the same Spirit, to another gifts of healing by that one Spirit, to another miraculous powers, to another prophecy, to another distinguishing between spirits, to another speaking in different kinds of tongues, and to still

another the interpretation of tongues. All these are the work of one and the same Spirit, and He distributes them to each one, just as He determines."

God created each of us with specific gifts and talents. They may be similar to someone else's gifts, because they are given by the same Holy Spirit. However, since each of us has been uniquely designed by God for His specific purpose, how we use His gifts will be displayed uniquely. Equipped with the knowledge of our gifts, we can begin to learn more about them, so we can use them to their fullest capacity for God's purpose. Learning to use our gifts will take study and practice; but we will also need the fruit of the Holy Spirit.

In *Galatians 5:22-25*, Paul teaches us about the fruit of the Spirit when he writes:

"But the fruit of the Spirit is love, joy, peace, forbearance, kindness, goodness, faithfulness, gentleness and self-control. Against such things there is no law. Those who belong to Christ Jesus have crucified the flesh with its passions and desires. Since we live by the Spirit, let us keep in step with the Spirit."

At first I wasn't sure that I had any fruit of the Spirit. Love, I never fully accepted it. Joy, never had it. Peace, what is that? Forbearance, had no clue what that meant. I wasn't a very kind person. Had limited experience with goodness. Faithfulness was a foreign concept. Gentleness, I was a tomboy. Self-control, well, I had to be in control always, in all ways. These were my views while I was in the darkness and I allowed the lies to control me. In His light, I have been given heavenly, unconditional love which allows me to give and receive love on a whole new level. I have a joy and peace that really does surpass all my understanding. Forbearance is when someone is patient and is able to deal with a difficult person or situation without becoming angry. Forbearance was a completely foreign concept to me; yet God's is developing this quality in me. I can give kindness and empathy because of my experiences with hurt, pain and brokenness. I have goodness only because He has given it to me. I know what gentleness is, because God has shown me His gentleness and I learning by His example. My self-control is now guided and lived out through God's words. As I have yielded myself to God's transforming process, He has produced the fruit of the Spirit in my life.

Are you ready to experience God's transforming process? Why?

_____

_____

_____

_____

_____

When we begin to truly live in the fullness of our God-created identity, and practice living by the fruits of the Spirit, the unlimited possibilities of God-confidence starts to shine.

Unlimited Possibilities with God-Confidence

The journey from broken to beautiful is a process to restore a shattered self-image, but it culminated in the discovery of God's image being formed in me. It is no longer about developing the self, self-image or self-confidence, it's about developing God's image in me and developing a God-confidence. It's not about us and our strength; it's about God's strength that empowers us. Discovering and developing our God-confidence starts with grace, humility, kindness and quiet strength.

Grace is beautiful. Many possible images come to mind when we hear the word-- the gracefulness of a dancer or the grace of a field of flowers blowing gently in the breeze. But the most beautiful picture of grace is recorded in *Romans 5:15* (AMP): *"But God's free gift is not at all to be compared to the trespass [His grace is out of all proportion to the fall of man]. For if many died through one man's falling away (his lapse, his offense), much more profusely did God's grace and the free gift [that comes] through the undeserved favor of the one Man Jesus Christ abound and overflow to and for [the benefit of] many."*

Grace, God's unmerited favor, comes in the form of God's

Son, Jesus. He is God's grace and free gift to us.

Humility is best described in *Proverbs 11:2 (AMP) "When swelling and pride come, then emptiness and shame come also, but with the humble (those who are lowly, who have been pruned or chiseled by trial, and renounce self) are skillful and godly wisdom and soundness."* When we are humble, chiseled by trial and willing to surrender ourselves to the Lord, we are positioned to receive wisdom. *Proverbs 16:18* warns us that *"pride goes before destruction, a haughty spirit before a fall"*; let's not allow pride and over-confidence ruin what God wants to accomplish through us.

Christ is the perfect example of kindness and through our redemption process, we have experienced His kindness. *Titus 3:4-6 "But when the kindness and love of God our Savior appeared, he saved us, not because of righteous things we had done, but because of his mercy. He saved us through the washing of rebirth and renewal by the Holy Spirit, whom he poured out on us generously through Jesus Christ our Savior."*

The definition of quiet strength is wrapped up in *Isaiah 30:15a (NLT) "This is what the Sovereign LORD, the Holy One of Israel, says: "Only in returning to me and resting in me will you be saved. In quietness and confidence is your strength."* When we return to Him out of our brokenness and decide to rest in Him, He gives us a quiet (yet mighty) strength, through His empowerment and confidence in us and this can take us far beyond what we could have ever imagined.

Are you ready to start seeing all the unlimited possibilities God has for you? Why?

_____

_____

_____

_____

_____

Sharing with you all the painful experiences along my path to restoration and transformation has been one of the hardest things I have ever done; but I wanted to walk in obedience on the path God prepared for me. I opened my journal and exposed my most intimate and raw emotions, my unfiltered communication with God. You entered into the darkest places where all the shattered, broken pieces of my failures, mistakes, shortcomings, unworthiness, worthlessness laid scattered all over the ground. I identified several of the accusing voices living in my head--fear, doubt, rejection, comparison and perfectionism. I acknowledged the mask I wore to cover my brokenness, the jagged pieces of pain I would not release, and all the lies about myself that I embraced. I have shared my story to encourage you that no matter how flawed or hopeless you feel, there is a glorious hope and extraordinary beauty waiting for you in God's arms. Surrender your broken, shattered life to God, because He can restore and transform you for His glory and for the blessing of others.

"Inaction breeds doubt and fear. Action breeds confidence and courage. If you want to conquer fear, do not sit home and think about it. Go out and get busy."[2] Dale Carnegie

Are you going to allow inaction to control your life? Keep you buried in the deep, dark pit? It's time to cast your doubt and fear aside and take action. No more playing it safe on the sidelines; it is time for you to put yourself into the race. Grant yourself forgiveness and forgive those who have hurt you so deeply. With God's help, restore and rebuild the places where trust was broken. Begin to trust the work God is doing in you and in your life. Give yourself permission to move forward by opening up your heart and taking risks. God has amazing things in store for you that exceed what your mind can conceive!

"Successful people maintain a positive focus in life no matter what is going on around them. They stay focused on their past successes rather than their past failures, and on the next action steps they need to take to get them closer to the fulfillment of their goals rather than all the other distractions that life presents to them."[3] Jack Canfield

God-sized dreams and purposes will require a positive focus on your part. Pray bigger than you have ever prayed before; open your eyes to amazing visions and God-sized dreams. He will give you the desires of your heart and show you unlimited possibilities. You will gaze in awestruck wonder as your beautiful, God-given purpose unfolds before you.

"Be inspired and encouraged to see the beautiful, confident, empowered woman God created you to be." Manda Hall

Your God kind of beauty is the realization, inspiration and encouragement to see what God can do and will do with that lumpy piece of black coal that is our lives. That lumpy of black coal represents a culmination of all the broken and shattered pieces of your heart and soul. He is the master creator and craftsman who hand–picked you. He will skillfully remove all dark places and reveal to you the beautiful, shiny and brilliant woman He had always intended for you to see and be.

Discover the gifts and talents God has placed in you, and then use them to inspire and encourage others. God will build your confidence in Him and He will wrap you up in grace, humility, kindness, patience, gentleness, tolerance and compassion.

The path to restoration is long, uncomfortable, and demanding, but the transformation that awaits you is bright, hopeful, magnificent and most importantly deserved. When you decide to surrender to God's restoring and transforming process, you have begun to restore that shattered self-image, going from broken and shattered, to a brilliant and beautiful woman.

Today is the day to take action and begin your own journey From Broken to Beautiful!

Acknowledgements

This book is dedicated first and foremost to God for giving me the courage, inspiration, and confidence to write this book--to expose my insecurities, brokenness and healing. For showing me that I have value and a purpose, Your Love for Me surpasses all my understanding, yet trusting in You has truly transformed my life!

To the amazing man God had planned for me, my husband Jason, who has loved me through it all from the age of 18 until now and beyond! We have battled, we have cried (well I have cried, lol), we have struggled, we have persevered, we are still passionate and have an incredible love! Thank you for loving me through all my imperfections, flaws, depression and self-doubt.

To my kids, Melanie and JJ, thank you for putting up with me during times when I wasn't the best mom; you loved and accepted me anyway! I love you both very much and I have cherished the opportunity to be your mom.

To the amazing ladies who impacted me: Maria Keckler, Leah Gowin, Carolyn Konecki, Rebecca Garcia, Betsy Ringer, Pam Farrel, Bobbye Brooks, and Beth Moseley. You saw the real me, believed in me when I didn't, accepted me for who I was flaws and all, and never judged me!!! For someone who never really had any girlfriends, you have all been a friend to me. You taught me how to be a friend. You were a shoulder to cry on, a sounding board, a kick in the pants. You gave me space when I needed it, but were always there to check on me when I pulled away. You have all inspired me and touched my heart in a profound way!

Notes

Chapter 3 – Living with the Voices

1. May, Robin. "The Truth about Perfection." Web log post. *Robin May Online*. 01 Apr. 2014. Web. 08 Oct. 2015.

Chapter 4 – Piece by Piece, One by One

1. "Piece By Piece by William Egan, Jr." Piece By Piece, a Poem by William Egan, Jr. All Poetry Poets. Accessed October 07, 2015. http://allpoetry.com/poem/5207423-Piece-By-Piece-by-WilliamEganJr.

Chapter 5 – Forgiving the Unforgivable

1. D'Amore, Josee. "Lori Stone Show." Interview by Lori Stone. Mountain Country 107.9. July 9, 2012.

Chapter 6 – Transformation is Possible

1. Big Daddy Weave, "Redeemed" www.azlyrics.com/lyrics/bigdaddyweave/redeemed.html
2. "Iyanla Vanzant Quotes." BrainyQuote. Accessed October 07, 2015. http://www.brainyquote.com/quotes/authors/i/iyanla_vanzant.html.
3. "Anna Quindlen Quote." BrainyQuote. Accessed October 07, 2015. http://www.brainyquote.com/quotes/quotes/a/annaquindl390536.html.

Chapter 7 – Our Hearts Must Go On

1. Christine Caine. *Unstoppable: Running the Race You Were Born to Win*. Grand Rapids, MI: Zondervan, 2014. 41.

2. Mark Batterson. *The Circle Maker: Praying Circles around Your Biggest Dreams and Greatest Fears*. Grand Rapids, MI: Zondervan, 2011. 62.
3. Mark Batterson. *The Circle Maker: Praying Circles around Your Biggest Dreams and Greatest Fears*. Grand Rapids, MI: Zondervan, 2011. 19.
4. Mark Batterson. *The Circle Maker: Praying Circles around Your Biggest Dreams and Greatest Fears*. Grand Rapids, MI: Zondervan, 2011. 137.
5. Mark Batterson. *The Circle Maker: Praying Circles around Your Biggest Dreams and Greatest Fears*. Grand Rapids, MI: Zondervan, 2011. 44.

Chapter 9 – Be God's Kind of Beautiful

1. "Leo Buscaglia Quote." BrainyQuote. Accessed October 07, 2015.http://www.brainyquote.com/quotes/quotes/l/leobuscagl150305.html.

2. "Dale Carnegie Quote." BrainyQuote. Accessed October 07, 2015.http://www.brainyquote.com/quotes/quotes/d/dalecarneg132157.html.

3. "Jack Canfield Quote." BrainyQuote. Accessed October 07, 2015. http://www.brainyquote.com/quotes/quotes/j/jackcanfie637648.html.

About the Author

Speaker, teacher and author, Manda Hall, is leading women from broken to beautiful by sharing her story and walking out God's purpose and plan for her life. Manda shares how she went from worthless to worthy, from the darkness of depression to the light of life, and from brokenness to God's beautiful daughter.

Manda's journey began with her national and then international daily outfit blog. Later she became a certified stylist, helping women rediscover their confidence through style. In the midst of her success, God expanded her vision from dressing the outsides, to addressing women's inner needs. She is passionate about leading women, who have experienced brokenness in their lives, into their rightful place as beautiful women whom God designed to enjoy lives of significance and meaning.

In 2014, she was honored by Hope for Women Magazine as one of their 25 Women Who Inspire.

Manda now shares and teaches on her message of From Broken to Beautiful, through workshops and speaking engagements.

Share in my daily adventures! Be sure to follow me on social media at:

https://instagram.com/mandahallministries/

https://www.facebook.com/mandahallministries

https://www.linkedin.com/in/mandahall

Invite Manda to Your Next Women's Event

Manda is passionate about inspiring and encouraging women to discover their true and real beauty. She knows from personal experience how hard it can be to start the journey out of deep dark pit of lies that keeps us from walking in the abundance God has for us. By sharing her personal journey with its setbacks and amazing victories, Manda will challenge the women in your group to start their own journey to from broken to beautiful.

Manda can be reached at info@mandahall.com or (866) 904-5370.

Testimonies

"I loved Manda's message. I so related with her story and how important is not to let fear paralyze us. Her testimony shows me how God can empower and TRANSFORM a woman into all He wants her to be. The ladies in our church were very blessed by her." *Carla Sparks, Women's Ministry HighPoint Church San Diego*

"Manda shared with the business women attending our luncheon about the importance of presenting and representing themselves in the marketplace as Christian Women Business Owners. Manda was knowledgeable, funny, left us feeling inspired to be better Christian business owner's and encouraged us to represent ourselves as the women God designed." *Debi McCaslin, President, Temecula Valley Women's Connection*

"Manda is a beautiful, transparent and inspirational speaker. This past year, 2014, we were richly blessed when Manda shared at our Fall Women's Retreat. In her message, Dress With Purpose, Manda shared personal stories and powerful scriptural truths to encourage us to become godly women of significance. Manda has a message women need to hear." *Cathy Horning, Co-Director of HER Ministry at Faith Community Church San Diego*

"Manda taught and encouraged the young women of Protect Your Heart Ministry, a ministry for young adult women who have aged out of the foster care system, about the value of how they treated their bodies and how to present themselves appropriately out in the world. Manda shared openly about her own personal struggles, dealing with her lack of self-worth and self-confidence. Manda was warm, compassionate and engaging with these young women, encouraging them to see beyond their circumstances and find their identity in Christ." *Rebecca Fox, Founder & Editor of Eve's Crown Magazine*

"We were so blessed to have Manda speak at the Women With Purpose Conference earlier this year. Her heart for helping women overcome obstacles and see themselves through God's eyes was evident as she shared her personal and very relatable story with us. We were engaged immediately as the women shared both tears and laughter together. Several women were talking about how much her talk meant to them. I highly recommend Manda as a speaker for your next women's event. I've invited her back myself to speak for me again at an upcoming women's retreat." *Rebecca Garcia, Coaching & Consulting Services and Founder & President of Christian Women Entrepreneurs Network*

MANDA HALL

Coming Soon

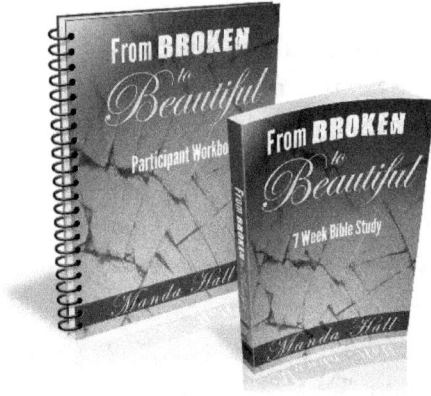

Bible study Course with Participant Workbook

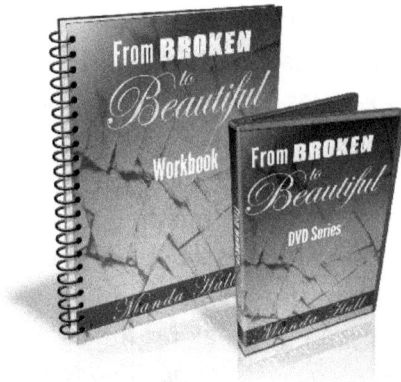

DVD Series and Workbook

www.ingramcontent.com/pod-product-compliance
Lightning Source LLC
LaVergne TN
LVHW051409080426
835508LV00022B/3012